GW01167763

I YOU HE SHE IT

GRIST

The Grist Anthology
2017

Experiments in Viewpoint

Published by University of Huddersfield Press

University of Huddersfield Press
The University of Huddersfield
Queensgate
Huddersfield HD1 3DH
Email enquiries university.press@hud.ac.uk

First published 2017

A CIP catalogue record for this book is available
from the British Library.
ISBN 978-1-86218-142-7
e-ISBN 978-1-86218-143-4
Designed by Carnegie Book Production
Printed by Jellyfish Solutions
COVER IMAGE: © Simon Crump 2017
Cover design and layout credited to Simon Crump and Mike Spikin
at the University of Huddersfield

University of
HUDDERSFIELD
Inspiring tomorrow's professionals

Contents

He

She

It

EDITORIAL TEAM

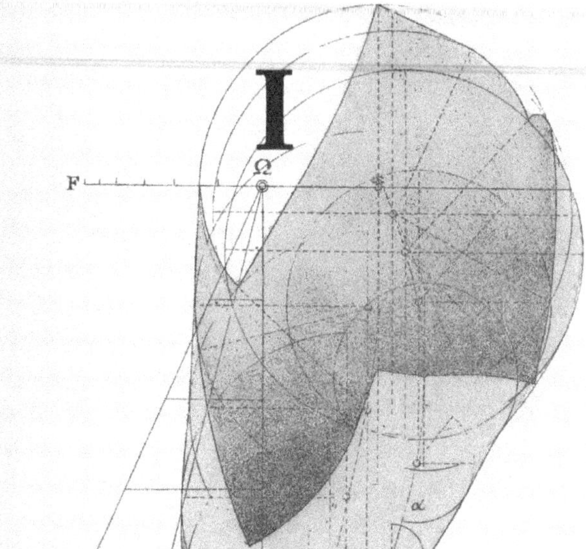
I
F
Ω
α
10·3
11·0

The Finest Cuts

LIAM BROWN

I TURNED THIRTEEN the summer Dad moved out to the car. It was an ancient Volvo, a rusting blue wreck that someone had rear-ended years ago and we'd never bothered to fix. Every morning he'd be waiting for me at the gate as I left for school, his shirt spilling out the back of his trousers, his suit as crumpled as the car's back bumper.

Sometimes Mum would stand watching from the doorstep, a cigarette throttled between bone-white knuckles, smoke leaking out between her gritted teeth. Though she never said a word, I could feel her eyes scorching the back of my blazer as Dad stooped to kiss me goodbye, my own eyes scrunched tight against the aniseed burn of his overproof breath.

As the days and weeks wore on, I began to see less and less of Dad. School had broken up for the holidays, and by the time I managed to drag myself from my bed in the morning, the Volvo would be gone, with only an oil-spotted patch of tarmac to signal that he'd been there at all. More than once I found myself shivering at my bedroom window with my face pressed to the glass, searching the darkness for the faint orange glow of his cigarette. I wondered if he was out there somewhere, looking back at me.

Summer inched towards autumn, and one morning I woke to realise I hadn't seen Dad in over a month. Life rumbled on all the same. I returned to school, finding myself a part-time job delivering papers in the evenings. Meanwhile Mum's boyfriend, Harry, started spending longer and longer at the house.

He would show up at dinnertime in his new Toyota, an over-buffed sports car with hideaway headlights and a private plate.

Truth be told, I didn't mind Harry too much. He worked as an advertising executive for an artificial flavourings company and most nights he would bring over samples of their latest experimental products for us to try, earnestly recording our responses on a checklist. I would sit at the dinner table and take tentative licks of chorizo-flavoured yoghurt or swig from a can of prawn cola while Harry sat around in Dad's old bathrobe, the belt loose around his waist to reveal a flash of sun-lamp shrivelled flesh each time he crossed his legs. For a while at least, the idiosyncratic contents of my lunchbox transformed me into a minor playground celebrity.

It was almost Christmas before Dad showed up again. The three of us were sat around after dinner one Friday evening, Mum and I chewing on sticks of venison bubble gum while Harry asked us questions about the flavour, consistency – whether or not we were experiencing any breathing difficulties – when the front door gave a solitary, shattering thump. Our house was never one to entertain unexpected callers, and as Mum rose from the table to investigate there was an air of unspoken dread that followed her. Only bad news would dare knock at this hour.

Harry was up from the table at the first sound of raised voices, my mother yelling about broken restraining orders and missed child support payments while I stayed in the kitchen, drumming my fingers on the counter and trying to scrape the rancid slick of synthetic deer from my tongue with my teeth. Eventually the clatter died down and Mum came back in to the room, Harry trailing sheepishly behind her.

"Your father would like to know if you'd like to spend the weekend with him?" she said, the words so clipped she almost swallowed them entirely.

"Now?" I asked.

"Tell him he doesn't have to go if he doesn't want to," Harry said, hissing at my mother through clenched porcelain veneers.

"Tell him no-one's forcing him. That man has no right turning up here like this, Helen."

"Jesus, Harry. He knows no-one's forcing him," she said, turning back to me. "You know no-one's forcing you, right?"

I stood there for a moment, my tongue still excavating my gums. Somewhere beyond the kitchen I heard the groan of a car door, an engine clearing its throat.

"I want to go," I said.

The inside of the car smelled like stale smoke and spilt beer, the forest of Magic Trees hanging from the stalk of the rear-view mirror doing little to mask the stink.

"Hey," said Dad.

"Hey."

"You hungry?"

"Uh-uh."

"Fine." Dad shrugged and released the handbrake.

Dad's new apartment was above a small Bangladeshi takeaway. The only way to enter was down a dingy alley that led to an ancient metal fire escape, the extractor fans at the back belching out a constant fug of singed aloo gobi and rancid ghee. The front door was jammed up with junk mail and old pizza boxes. Dad had to pin it back with his shoulder while I scrambled through the gap under his arm into a grimy bedsit, the sink in the corner overflowing with festering cups, a stained sheet strung across the window to act as a curtain.

"I haven't got round to picking up a bed yet," he said as he closed the door and hit the light switch, a bare 40 watt bulb spilling a jaundiced glow across the carnage. "You've got the chair or the floor."

I glanced down at the wood effect vinyl, noticing the loose topsoil of old tobacco, matted hair and broken glass.

"I'll take the chair," I said.

I woke to the sound of bacon spitting. Thin winter sunlight poured in through the gap between the sheet and the window. As I sat up and rubbed the crust from my eyes I saw the room looked a little sharper somehow, the coffee table clammy from a recent wiping. At the foot of the chair I noticed a long canvas sack.

Dad was whistling as he came over, a breakfast balanced in each enormous hand.

"I thought we'd go camping," he said, handing me a plate of blackened bacon and eggs.

"Today?" I asked. Despite the sunshine there was a chill in the air; the skin on my arm puckered even indoors.

Dad's smile flickered slightly as he gripped the brown sauce bottle, "Why, are you doing something else today?"

I shook my head, "No."

"Well then."

"It's just... It's winter."

Dad smiled again, "What are you? A man or a mouse?"

This was a trick, a question he used to ask back when I was a kid whenever I'd moan about tidying my bedroom or mowing the lawn.

I made a squeaking sound and wrinkled my nose.

By the time we'd dressed and loaded the car it was almost midday. Most of the real camping equipment was still packed away in boxes in Mum's garage, so we had to improvise with bits and pieces scavenged from around the apartment. Pans and cutlery from the stagnant washing up bowl. Half a bag of Doritos and a fresh case of Carlsberg. The tent was on loan from one of Dad's old drinking buddies, Denny, who was apparently something of a keen angler.

"Not that he's ever caught squat," Dad said with a laugh as he swung the boot shut. "Nothing except hepatitis, anyway."

The traffic was bad for a Saturday and my stomach growled as we crawled down the high street, Dad chain smoking out the window.

"Can we stop and get a bite?" I asked, nodding towards a McDonalds a little down the street.

"There?" Dad asked, turning his attention away from the pensioner he was mid-way through giving the finger to. "Have you ever considered the amount of crap they pump into that stuff? Franken-burgers they call 'em. Kind of things that Harry

Palmer and his pals cook up in their fancy lab I wouldn't wonder."

I didn't say anything after that. It was the first time I'd heard Dad use Harry's name. It felt strange, as if a small but dangerous animal had crawled through the window and fallen asleep on the back seat. I didn't want to be the one to wake it.

A little while later Dad pulled the car over to the side of the road and hit the hazards. Then, without a word, he unhitched his seatbelt and got out. A few minutes later he was back, a small sack of charcoal over his shoulder and a lumpy white bag gripped tightly in his fist.

"You ever had a dirty steak son?" he asked.

I shook my head.

He grinned, "Your grandad used to cook 'em up all the time when I was a kid. Used to freak Nana out something rotten. What you do is you take yourself a couple of T-bones," he paused to shake the bag. "Nice tender, butcher's cuts. None of that vacuum-sucked supermarket muck. After that, you build yourself a nice big fire. You can't cheat on that bit neither. No petrol or paraffin blocks, else you'll poison yourself. Once you've got your fire nice and hot you add your charcoal, wait for the lumps to glow, then toss your steaks on top. No oil, no seasoning. Just meat and fire the way God intended." Dad laughed, tossing the bag of steak into my lap. "Wonder what Harry Palmer would have to say about that, huh?"

The traffic thinned out as we left the city. Dad didn't like listening to music while he drove so we kept the radio tuned to the football, the penalties and off-side calls interrupted by increasingly large yawns of static as the signal faded, until eventually we lost the commentary altogether. After that we sat in silence, eating Doritos and listening to the rattle and squeak of the Volvo's suspension on the pockmarked gravel, each lost to our own thoughts.

"That a Toyota he's got?"

I swallowed hard, Dad's question yanking me back into the present.

"Hmmm?"

"Red one, up on your Mum's drive. What is it? An MR2"

I shrugged.

Dad cleared his throat, unrolled the window a couple of inches and sent a missile of spit streaking into the wind.

"Never liked Toyotas," he said as he wound it back up. "Poor man's Ferrari if you ask me."

I didn't mention the disconcerting rattle coming from the undercarriage of the Volvo.

It was almost dark by the time Dad pulled off the track and killed the engine. I peered into the trees, trying to imagine where we might set a tent. It was impossible to see more than a few feet into the dense thicket.

"Come on then!" Dad said, as he reached for the door. "Are you a man or a mouse?"

I gave a small, dutiful squeak.

We seemed to walk for a long time. It was hard going, with brambles tearing at our ankles and mossy stumps rearing up out of the darkness, the perfect height to jar a shin or crack an unsuspecting kneecap. Several times we had to stop to scramble around blindly amongst the dead leaves and dirt to retrieve items that had slipped from our grasp. Indeed, the light was so bad I could hardly make out Dad a few feet in front of me, with only the dim glow from his cigarette leading the way.

Eventually we came to a small clearing and staggered to a halt. Dad dropped the bags and immediately cracked a beer to celebrate.

"Didn't I tell you?" he asked.

I nodded, hoping he couldn't make out my expression in the dark.

My job was to pitch the tent while Dad gathered wood for the fire. My hands were so cold that it was hard to get the bag's zipper open. When I eventually did, I knew at once it wasn't going to work. It was a dome tent, a two-man, but even in the dark I could see there was something missing. No matter how many times I flipped over the canvas or rethreaded the pole through the meshed fabric of the inner flaps, I couldn't get the thing to slot together. I was still standing over it when Dad returned, his arms laden with branches.

"What are you...?" he snapped, but quickly stopped as he stooped to examine the crumpled debris at my feet. "You're missing a pole. Have you checked the bag?"

"I've checked," I said.

"Well check again."

Dad stayed on the ground for a couple more minutes, fiddling with the canvas before letting it slump to the floor.

"That bastard Denny," he said, more to himself than to me. "He said he used it just this summer."

I stood there, shivering under my coat. I didn't know what to say.

As if waking from a trance, Dad clapped his hands together.

"It's fine," he said. "We can just sleep under it like that, army-style. It'll be like a big sleeping bag. We'll get the fire going and everything will be just fine. Sleeping out under the stars with your old man huh? Now that's what I call an adventure."

I nodded as Dad laughed and cracked another can. Glancing up, I couldn't help noticing there wasn't a single star in the sky.

Dad spent about half an hour meticulously laying out the wood, talking me through the process as he first raked out a bare soil bed with his hands, then placed a springy ball of dry leaves and grass in the centre. I watched as he built a small tepee around it with pencil-thin twigs, leaving one side open so that the air could get in and feed the fire. Finally, he stacked the larger branches around the outside and then pushed his hand through the gap, holding his lighter to the bundle. I leant closer, watching as the grass smouldered and popped under the flame. Yet it refused to take. As the minutes passed Dad's movements became less precise. He jabbed the lighter towards the branches and several times the pile collapsed. He dropped to his chest and began huffing into the smoking leaves, curse words escaping with every breath.

"It's wet," Dad said, taking a stick from the pile. It bent but didn't snap. "Did it rain this week?"

The question sounded like a threat.

I kept very still, staring into the heap and willing it to catch.

And then, quite unexpectedly, it did.

At once Dad redoubled his efforts, circling the fire and steadily blowing as the ball of tinder glowed first orange then blue, the flames at last creeping upwards and licking the kindling. In no time at all the fire was roaring. Dad stood proudly back, draining a can and reaching for another.

"What did I tell you?" he said. "Isn't this great?"

Basking in the warm bubble of light, it was hard to argue with him. The fire had transformed the clearing completely, casting strange, crooked shadows all around us. It was as if a flickering spotlight had been suspended above our heads, illuminating this single perfect spot amongst the endless acres of darkness. As if we were chosen, somehow.

"Right, time to eat," Dad said after a couple of minutes. The light and heat instantly faded as he shook the coals over the fire, but I was too hungry to complain. I felt around in the shadows until I found the bag of meat, tearing open the polythene. I was hit immediately by the sour stink of ammonia. Tilting the bag, I saw how the surface of the steak glinted green in the dull light.

"Dad... I don't think these are right."

He was over at once, all brag and bluster as he snatched the bag from my grip. He lowered his face to take a sniff, then jerked away as he retched violently, a string of drool swaying from his open mouth.

It was a while before he straightened up, and even once he had he didn't say anything. He just stood there, staring at the bad meat, a crinkle of disbelief on his brow, almost lost amongst all the other lines and creases. Then all at once his body seemed to stiffen, a white anger boiling through him as he took a couple of steps backwards and, with a roar, pitched the bag high into the air.

There was a soft crack somewhere above us. Looking up we saw the bag had snagged on a low branch just overhead. Blood was already trickling through the shredded plastic. In the dying light we stood together and watched it drip.

It's a funny thing to hear an adult cry. No matter how big or old or broken they are, they always sound like children. That night as I lay shivering under the canvas, I heard the wavering high-pitched whimper of my father weeping. I'd gone to bed long before him, leaving him to his beer and the fire while I coiled myself in what was left of the tent. I didn't sleep though. Rather, I lay there with my eyes closed as the unfamiliar, private sounds of the forest unfolded all around me.

I was still awake hours later when Dad leant over and shook me. Acting on some long-forgotten impulse, however, I feigned sleep, keeping my eyes shut and my body stubbornly limp. He sighed, swore, shook me again. Still I didn't move. Then, with a strength I'd long forgotten he possessed, I felt him squat beside me and slide his hands under my ribs, hoisting me out from under the fabric and into his arms. And even as he staggered through the undergrowth, gasping under the weight of me as he headed back to the car, and later to the city, to Mum and Harry, I kept my head still against his shoulder and my eyes squeezed tight, listening to him struggle as he carried me like a child, deep into the night.

At Last

POPPY CONNOR-SLATER

I FLINCHED AS the freezing water began to spill over my wellies but I carried on wading in. A flock of oystercatchers that were bobbing up and down on the surface nearby were startled by my splashing and took off in a flurry of black and white, piping their alarm calls. The further in I got the harder it was to drag my legs through the water. When it hit my chest I felt almost winded by the cold and had to take a moment to breathe, and then I began to swim. Finally, I scrunched up my eyes and ducked below the surface.

At first when I opened my eyes the water stung them so much that all I could make out was a blur of the light coming from above. As I tried to blink the stinging away, the murky world began to come into focus and then I could see them – their shapes emerging from the dark. I stretched out my hands towards them.

As we pulled onto the dirt track all I could think about was my new sandals that were tucked up inside my suitcase in the boot of the car. They were shiny and black with a tiny heel and they were so beautiful. I looked out of the window at the dark water and the endless scrub that eventually jutted up into great mountains. What was the point in pretty sandals here?

"Look, you can see Grandma's house now," said Dad, gesturing to a cluster of little white houses that perched on the edge of the loch. We crept slowly down the track towards the water in silence until dad said, "You alright, Kat?"

I nodded, and turning to him saw that his eyes were red. I quickly looked back to the window.

We pulled up in front of the houses and dad turned off the engine. He hesitated for a moment and then tried to look me in the eye.

"Sure you're ok?"

I nodded again.

"Ok. Let's go in, shall we?"

As soon as I opened the car door the wind hit me, making my hair whip in my face and stick to my lip gloss. Dad went to the boot to lift out our suitcases and then knocked on the door of the cottage. It opened to reveal my grandma, wearing a flowery dress that I could remember from when I was almost a baby.

"Tony! Come in, come in," she said as she drew dad in for a hug. She ushered him inside and then pulled me to her. "Oh, Kit-Kat, I think you grow a foot every time I see you!" Grandma smelled like baking. I wondered if there would be fresh bread and fairy cakes. There always used to be.

"You can have the spare room, Kat," she whispered with a wink. "Your dad's been demoted to the sofa."

"I heard that!" Dad called from down the hall. "Come on, I'll help you take your case up."

I followed him up the narrow staircase into a small, bright room. I could see the camping mattress that I used to sleep on folded up underneath the bedframe. I clambered onto the bed and looked out of the window.

"Gorgeous view, eh?" Dad said.

I could see Dad's car and Grandma's car, and then behind that a little path that led down to the pebble beach. The loch stretched on forever – so far that the mountains on the other side were a pale blue.

"If you had a boat and sailed in that direction," Dad said, gesturing to the right, "you'd get to the sea after only five miles or so. Maybe we could all have a drive down sometime this week."

I ignored him and continued to stare out of the window. Dad sighed and rubbed the back of his neck.

"Look, Kat. I know that you wanted to stay in London and spend Easter with your friends. I'm just trying to do what's best. I'm sorry, ok?"

"Dad, I'm fine," I snapped.

"Ok. Ok. Well, I'll leave you to unpack your stuff then, love," he said, and headed back downstairs.

I waited a few moments and then crept to the top of the stairs. I could just hear the murmur of voices drifting up from the living room.

"She's still awful quiet," I heard Grandma say.

"I know. She barely talks to me," Dad answered. "And then bringing her here... all I could think of on the drive was all of the times we'd made the journey before. With Sally. Maybe I've done the wrong thing." I heard a stifled sob and I gritted my teeth.

"Tony, Tony," Grandma stammered, "it's ok. I think this will be good for us all, in the end."

That night when I turned off my light it was so dark that I couldn't see my hand when I waved it in front of my face, even when I opened my eyes as wide as they would go. It was strange, almost as if I wasn't properly a part of my body. As I lay there I thought that I could hear the sound of gently lapping water floating in through the window.

In the morning I woke to see that a heavy fog had descended overnight, covering my window with a haze of tiny water droplets. I pulled a jumper on over my pyjamas and traipsed downstairs. Grandma was already in the kitchen, sitting at the table with a cup of tea. She smiled and got to her feet when she saw me.

"Morning, love. Let me get you a hot drink. Tea?"

"Please," I replied, rubbing my eyes.

Grandma set about boiling the kettle and pulling boxes of cereal out of a cupboard.

"I'll make one for your dad, too, in case he wakes up", she said as she set a box of Frosties in front of me. "We're going to go to town to get some shopping today. You can come if you like. We might get chips and eat them on the harbour."

"Maybe," I said as Grandma handed me my tea.

Over breakfast, Grandma asked me about school and if I was still taking dance classes, and then launched into a long story about how she'd had to help her neighbour rescue a baby cow that had got stuck in some deep mud.

"You always used to like animals, didn't you?" she asked.

"I guess so," I said.

"We've had so many seals along the loch recently. If you go and sit out there for an hour, I can promise that you'll see at least one. Sweet little things," she said as she stood and began to clear away the breakfast things. "Have you ever heard of selkies, pet?"

"No," I answered.

"Well, there's a little folktale around here that says they're these creatures that are a bit like mermaids. In the water they're seals – just like any other ordinary seal. But then when they come out of the water they shed their sealskin and take on the shape of a human."

I looked at her in surprise.

"I know, I know," she said. "It's a bit strange. My mam used to tell me that those we love who have passed on become selkies and watch over us. You know, a bit like angels."

Grandma smiled to herself as she leaned on the sideboard and gazed out of the window. I wondered if she was thinking about mum, living as some magical creature in the icy black water of the loch. I wished she'd never said anything.

I stayed behind when Grandma and dad went to get shopping. Grandma left me some sandwiches in the fridge and gave me a key in case I wanted to go for a walk, but said I wasn't to go too far. I lay on my bed and tried to read a book, but I just kept reading the same paragraph over and over again without the words going in. Then I tried to text my friend Laura but I only had one bar of signal and it kept failing to send. I knelt on my bed and looked out of the window. The mist was beginning to thin and I could see sunlight trying to break through it. Maybe I would go for a walk like Grandma had said. I went to the cupboard where I'd put all of my clothes. My sandals were sat there at the bottom, looking out of place. I'd only had a chance to wear them twice so far. I sighed and picked up the Converse that were laid next to them.

The mist was almost gone completely by the time I got out of the house. I trudged down the grit path that led down to the pebble beach and then looked both ways, trying to decide which way to walk. I decided to go left, where I could see the bank pulling away from the beach and turning into cliffs. There was barely a breeze and the loch was very still, only lapping very slightly at the pebbles on the beach.

Once I had walked for a while, kicking pebbles as I went, and had put some distance between myself and the house, I stopped and found a rock to sit on. It was so quiet. No cars, no aeroplanes, no nothing. Out of the corner of my eye I saw a rounded shape disturb the stillness of the water. My heart began to beat a little faster and a forgotten excitement tried to stir inside me as I saw that a seal had poked its head above the surface only a few metres from the water's edge. Its shining, fluid body bobbed up and down, and then was joined by a second seal that appeared as if from nowhere. I held every muscle in my body as still as I could and barely dared to breathe. The seals looked in my direction for a minute or two, and I could see beads of water clinging to their whiskers, and then they continued their journey along the loch until I couldn't see them any more.

When I let myself into the cottage an hour or two later Dad and Grandma were already home.

"Look at your pretty white trainers! You've got mud all over them!" Grandma cried, "are these the most durable shoes you've got?"

I nodded, startled.

"What size shoe are you, pet?"

"Five" I replied.

"Ok, here, you can use my wellies", Grandma said, bustling over to the shoe rack, "they're a six but they'll be fine if you wear thick socks. I'll put them by the door for you. Now come with me and tell me about your day. Did you see a seal?"

Before I'd realised what I was doing I'd told Grandma all about the seals – described their large eyes and whiskery noses and the way that they almost seemed to be made of the same stuff as the loch, and then I saw dad watching us from the doorway with a small smile on his face.

"Uh. Well, I've got some stuff to do. Homework," I mumbled and headed for my room.

I woke up early the next day even though I hadn't set an alarm. Grandma and Dad were both still asleep, so I quietly got myself some breakfast. Once I'd eaten I went to the front door and looked at the shoes all lined up. The wellies Grandma had lent me were a dull green and were dusted with dried mud. I pulled them on, wrapped myself in my coat and opened the door. It was windy today, and cold. I huddled into my coat as I made my way to the beach. I found a spot that was a little sheltered from the wind by the cliff and settled myself down. The water was steel grey and the wind was lifting it up in little peaks. Today the absence of human sounds seemed strangely loud. The sound of water on the pebbles, the wind on the waves and in the trees, and birds calling in the scrub behind me filled up my mind like white noise.

The sound of crunching pebbles startled me and I looked up to see Dad looking half asleep.

"I was worried about you," he said as he reached me, "didn't know where you were!"

"Just getting some fresh air," I said, as I tried to bury deeper into my coat.

"Grandma said she thought you might be out here. Looking for seals?"

I stared across the water in silence.

"Here, I found these in the house," Dad said as he handed me a pair of binoculars. "You'll be able to see them better."

I took them from him and held them to my eyes. The blurry circles sharpened as I turned the focus dial and then I could see the houses on the other side of the loch – I could even make out flowers in a window box and the shape of a bird table in someone's garden.

"Don't stay out too long, ok, love? You'll get cold. I'm making lunch for about one."

I nodded at him and he took a moment to contemplate the loch before turning back toward the house. I leaned back against the cliff and focused the binoculars on the water and scanned around. The waves formed dark shapes all over the loch that I kept mistaking for creatures. I began to feel dizzy from the constant motion and set the binoculars down. I closed my eyes for a few moments and concentrated on the solidity of the ground beneath me. When I opened my eyes again I saw a group of seals making their way leisurely down the loch towards me, bobbing in and out of the water as they went. I quickly lifted the binoculars back to my eyes and tried to find the seals. Their dappled skin glistened in the grey light and they puffed sprays of water from their noses after they'd been under the surface. As they got nearer, one of them seemed to see me and stopped to have a look, and the others stopped soon after.

I lowered the binoculars and hooked the chord around my neck before I began to edge closer to the water, trying to move as quietly as possible. The first seal stayed suspended in the water, still staring. The others backed away slightly but seemed just as curious. Once I'd managed to get a couple of metres from the water's edge I lowered myself gently onto the pebbles. We regarded each other for what felt like a long time, and all of the sounds that had surrounded me before now faded away. Their eyes were as alert and expressive as a human's, and I felt almost as if we could have started talking to each other. Eventually the first seal broke the stillness and turned to look at the others. They all began to carry on in the direction that they had been going in, but they looked back a few times, as if still curious about me.

I came back to the beach every day and waited by the edge of the loch until the seals appeared. There was a different number every time, but there was always one seal in particular that stopped to look at me. Every day they got closer, and I felt like they had begun to expect me.

Dad had started to come down to the beach to bring me biscuits and flasks of hot tea, which I welcomed as the air was so bitter, but he never stayed for long. He said that he could see me from the kitchen window. Sometimes he and Grandma went out on walks or to town, but I preferred to stay by the loch.

Two days before we were due to go home I went out as the sun was rising and sat in my usual spot on the beach. I waited patiently for hours but the seals didn't appear. I wouldn't go inside without seeing them so Dad had to bring me my lunch outside. I didn't feel like eating. The time went on and on and I went through countless flasks of tea and not one seal appeared in the water. Eventually the light began to drop and I could hear blackbirds singing their evening song and I had to go inside because my fingers were going numb. Dad and Grandma both came to the hall as I opened the door but I avoided their eyes, ran past them without taking off my coat or wellies, and went up into my bedroom and closed the door behind me before they could say anything.

All night I never felt quite awake or quite asleep. I just turned over and over while strange images and voices rushed through my head until I woke up, confused, in the bright daylight. I could hear the sound of the television downstairs and a noisy family walking by outside, and I realised it must be at least mid morning. I looked out of the window and saw that the sky was lined with heavy clouds, but that the sun was breaking through, lighting them up like a paper lampshade and making the loch shimmer.

I got out of bed and pulled my coat and wellies on right over my pyjamas before making my way downstairs.

"Kat?" Grandma called as she and Dad appeared in the living room doorway. "Let me get you some tea! Would you like breakfast?"

I ignored her and made my way to the front door and out onto the path. I heard Dad's heavy steps coming after me.

"Kat, won't you eat something? You didn't have dinner! Where are you going?" he shouted after me.

"Leave me alone!" I spat over my shoulder. Dad's footsteps stopped and I ran down to the beach alone.

I huddled at the edge of the loch with my knees drawn up to my chin, not taking my eyes from the rippling surface of the loch. Sometimes I heard people passing on the beach, and once Grandma came to try and get me to come inside, but I never once looked away.

When I felt like I'd been sitting there for an eternity something flickered in the periphery of my vision. A shiver ran through my body as I saw three seals swimming towards me at last. I rushed forwards almost involuntarily and splashed right into the waves.

Just as my fingertips brushed the seal's silky nose I felt the water drag my body down and around, knocking the air out of my lungs until I wasn't sure which way up I was. A stream of bubbles coming from my own mouth obscured my vision and I couldn't see the seals or the surface any more. The panic made my head swim and my blood pounded loud in my ears.

Then I felt a fog begin to flower in my brain and the noise and the whirling slowed and stopped all together. From within the haze of bubbles and fractured light I saw brown eyes smiling at me I and felt a soft hand on my cheek. I smiled back as the world began to slowly dissolve.

Someone was shouting my name when my head broke the surface. I gasped huge lungfuls of air even though salty water droplets burnt my throat. Big hands were dragging me through the water and the roaring of the air and the world surrounded me. I looked up and saw Dad's pale frowning face. When the water became shallower he lifted me up completely and I wrapped my arms tight around his neck.

Now that I was above the surface the water looked deceptively calm. I stared at it over Dad's shoulder, willing myself to be able to see through the grey waves.

"It's ok. you're ok," he mumbled.

The wind bit my damp skin and I began, at last, to cry.

Greyhound

MATILDE CHRISTENSEN

I PUT MY bag over my shoulder as the bus approaches the bay. WINNIPEG it says with dull, yellow letters on the front. The evening is wet and dreary; the raindrops drain through my hair and cool down my scalp as I wait for the bus driver to open the doors.

I'm more than glad to finally leave this godforsaken bus depot behind. I shudder and take the three steps into the cabin. It's nice and warm in here, and I walk down to the very back to find two unoccupied seats. I go on the coach all the time and I prefer to have two seats to myself; I guess everyone does. We've all been taught to keep away from strangers.

The bus is not that crowded, yet it still smells too much like people. Two decent-looking blondes are sitting a couple of rows ahead of me. They obviously don't spare me a look. They're talking excitedly about something, probably the news. The guy who killed his seatmate on a coach trip from Edmonton to Winnipeg six years ago was recently released. Since, the story has been all over TV and on everyone's lips. Apparently he was a schizophrenic. Ate parts of the victim's face after sawing his head off with a Rambo knife. You hear all sorts of things. I sit back in my seat. What was his name? Vince Lee? These long distance rides are so immensely mind-numbing they're borderline torturous. Can't say I'm surprised that someone cracked.

Unlike the shrieking girls in the front I'm really not that bothered. I'm sure that Lee, or whatever his name is, is sitting comfortably at home, doped up on his meds, while I'm gonna be stuck on here for a good five hours. To entertain myself I always bring the same few things: an issue of *Gun Dog Magazine*, two bags of travel sweets (one bag of Skittles, one bag of M&Ms), a can of soda (usually Coke, but the convenience store only had Pepsi) and my mp3-player. This kind of thing quickly becomes a ritual.

I go to Winnipeg to visit friends and family; I grew up around there. Tomorrow I'm going fishing with my dad. As soon as the bus starts moving I plug in my headset and close my eyes. I like to listen to classical music while driving out of town. Mozart, Chopin; it soothes me and makes me doze off.

I usually sleep the first hour until we hit the highway, and surely enough, just as always, the soft tones of 'Piano Concerto No. 4' makes my body sink deeper into the seat. 'G Major'. Deeper yet. And slowly sleep envelopes me in colorful, coffee-stained plush.

I'm woken up by a crescendo. The shock of the high pitched keys has sent the adrenaline rushing through my body. My head is resting on the ice-cold window. Condensation has formed on half my face. As I sit up I realise someone is now sitting next to me. We must have stopped in Russell to pick up more passengers. This is not unusual.

He has put my backpack on the floor, and it annoys me a little. Surely there were other seats available. I steal a glance at the man; he's wearing a cap. Looks like an alright guy, I guess. Doesn't take up too much space either. I hate those armrest-Nazis that try to conquer your seat with their fat thighs and elbows. I switch off the music and take my headset off.

The bag of M&Ms gives a promising rattle as I retrieve it from my backpack. I shake out a handful and pour back the ones that aren't red. I eat the remaining, one by one. Then I shake out another handful and pour back the ones that aren't red. With my thumb and index finger I rummage through the bag catching the last few red ones while counting them: one, two three, four, five, six. All that's left is a multi-coloured anarchy that I'm not the least bit interested in. I offer the bag to my seatmate, thinking that we may as well get acquainted now that we're spending the next few hours trapped in this shoe box together. He briefly meets my eyes, smiles and shakes his head. He seems remarkably familiar; must be one of those faces.

I put the bag away as I turn to look out the window. My reflection is obscure. Before I start to search my brain for an answer to where I've seen this guy before, I contemplate whether it's worth my time. I decide that it isn't. Yet, I have that feeling of knowing, but not knowing, that makes your brain sort of itchy, and you know it will drive you mad if you don't scratch it.

So I start to think, staring into the darkness on the other side of the glass. Did he go to my school? The area around here is flat and swampy; sometimes I see the reflection of yellow squares in the black waters next to the road. I sit back in my seat, trying to sneak a peek at him. He's just sat there with his eyes fixed on the back of the seat in front of him as if he's counting the little red triangles of the pattern in the plush. I say that because I once did so myself; 182.

It sort of dawns on me slowly. A line of associations seem to plunge me inch by inch into a well of cold water. Suddenly I break out in a sweat. I am almost entirely sure... but it can't be. I take another look out of the corner of my eye and there's no denying it; he looks strikingly like the guy whose face has been all over TV. That guy. Vince Lee.

At first I try to stay calm. I could be mistaken. Surely they wouldn't let him back on the bus. Fighting the desire to flee I fidget in my seat and cross my legs, knocking his knee with my foot as I do so.

"Sorry," I say with the driest throat, halfway expecting him to pounce on me. Nothing happens. What the hell am I supposed to do now? Should I notify someone? Are we all in danger? If I could just get out of my seat and off the bus at the next stop. I look at my watch as casually as I can manage. We aren't supposed to stop for another two hours.

I find myself panicking. My heart is racing and it takes all my will power to keep my breathing under control. Believing I can feel the warmth from his body creep through the fabric of my shirt and onto my skin makes me slink closer to the wall. My neck cramps up as I force myself to look straight out the window, my head turned in an awkward angle, as far away from him as possible. Outside, lonely gas stations and desolate houses rush by like white ghosts against a starless sky.

I'm painfully aware of every move my seatmate is making. I hear the bumps of his knees against the seat in front; the friction as he slides his wrist over the armrest; the sound of rubber soles shuffling on the dirty floor. Everyone else seems to have gone quiet, as if all other passengers have left the bus at Russell. I take a quick look around; the bus is full of empty seats. I'm struck by a terrifying revelation; out of all the empty rows this guy sits next to me. Why? Has he made me his target? Lee or not, this guy is a raving lunatic. The idea of being trapped alone with him on a bus, in the middle of fucking nowhere, makes me feel sick with fear.

I crouch against the window. A creepy-crawly sensation travels over my skin and for a moment I'm certain I can sense his breathing on the back of my neck.

Compulsively I turn around, convinced that he is inches away from grabbing me – but he just sits there with his hands folded in his lap, looking out of the window. He smiles at me again. I force myself to reciprocate.

After what seems like an eternity of clinging to the window pane, the bus pulls into a gas station and the lights are turned up in the cabin. A rustle breaks loose as people seem to reappear in their seats and the bus driver calls down the aisle that we've stopped for gas.

Relieved to at least not be alone I sit back in my seat; with the lights on I feel like I've just woken up from a nightmare. I quickly glance at my seatmate; I hadn't realised he had fallen asleep. Studying his face a little closer I decide that I was mistaken; this is not the guy from the news who killed someone on a bus. I mean, how could it be? Certainly he must have been placed in some sort of halfway house at this point. What an idiot I am for actually believing that it was him. I take a few deep breaths, feeling my pulse calming down and my shoulders easing up.

The engine starts humming beneath my feet again and we leave the gas station behind us. Back on the road the darkness once more creeps up on me; the roads are so damn quiet at this time of night and there's a long way between the light posts.

I switch on the little lamp above my head; it cloaks me in a cone of light. I get the can of Pepsi out of my bag, thinking it a good way of distracting myself. I drink it while reading *Gun Dog;* there's an article on greyhound breeding schemes and for a moment I lose myself in reading.

"Can I borrow that when you're done?"

I jerk my head to the side, surprised by the words spoken close to my ear. The guy next to me has woken up from his nap and is now reading *Gun Dog* over my shoulder.

"Y-yes," I say. Now that he's awake and animated he once more fills me with that unwelcome feeling of familiarity.

"Just in your own time," he says, leaning back with a smile. His facial expression changes into one of concern as he adds, "are you alright?"

I realise I must have been staring at him for an inappropriately long time and I snap myself out of it.

"Yes, fine. I'm fine," I say. For some reason sweat is forming on my upper lip.

Suddenly he grins and leans towards me, "Don't worry, I ain't planning on killing anyone else anytime soon."

An untimely 'ha-ha' escapes my throat like croaks from a frog. Feeling the color drain from my face I stare into his dark eyes; he is dead earnest. A sudden jerk of his arm makes me flinch; he's pointing a finger gun straight in my face.

"Gotcha!" He starts laughing loudly: "You should see your face, man."

I try to laugh, but nothing really comes out.

"Relax, buddy. I was only messing with ya," he says while patting my shoulder. "The resemblance is striking, ay? There's no way they would let that guy back on a bus through. I personally think they should have ended him then and there, but I guess we're not in America."

"I guess not," I say. My heart is still pounding in my chest and I discreetly rub my palms on my thighs, wiping the sweat off on my jeans.

I feel somewhat embarrassed. I can't have been the only person mistaking him for Lee over the past few weeks. Thinking about it, I can't blame the guy for wanting to sit next to someone in order to blend in a little more. We sit quietly for a moment, driving through a dead Minnedosa.

"Do you know how he did it?" my seatmate suddenly asks.

I look at him, "Yes," I say.

My seatmate pretends to hold a head by the hair while sawing at its neck with an imaginary knife.

"Yes," I say again.

"He must have been a stubborn fucker," my seatmate says, "chopping a head off like that. Not that you can blame him. It's a hard job keeping yourself entertained on a bus."

I don't like where this is heading. I don't like that he's talking to me as if we're buddies, or something other than complete strangers.

"Did you wanna borrow this?" I quickly ask to shut him up, handing over my half-read issue of *Gun Dog*. Without looking at it he takes it, saying "thanks". He puts it in his lap.

"I wonder what made him do it," he says. "Do you think you would be capable of doing something like that?"

I'm resenting this conversation. In fact, I'm resenting getting on this damn bus in the first place. Should have taken an earlier coach; the weirdos always come out at night.

"I don't know," I say.

"I'm sure you would," he says, "if you had the motivation to do it."

"I doubt it." "Don't be modest."

"Modest!" I stare at him.

He just grins.

"Do you find this funny?" The words sort of just spurt out of me. Quite frankly, I'm getting a little fed up with this guy.

"Just making conversation," my seatmate says, gesturing with his hands.

"This is morbid!"

"Oh, don't be like that."

"Just... Leave me alone, please," I say, crossing my arms and closing my eyes, pretending to go to sleep. Who the hell is this guy, and what is he doing sitting here annoying me? I can live with him forcing his presence on me, stealing my extra seat, but for the love of God, why doesn't he just shut up?

He must have taken the hint though; he's gone quiet and after a few minutes I almost forget that he's there. The gentle rocking of the coach soothes me. On the verge of slumber I float in and out of little dreams about trains and running dogs.

I'm bumped back into consciousness as a wheel goes in a pothole. I open one eye, just to check on him. He's sitting, slightly bent over, fiddling with something. Probably reading my *Gun Dog*, I think to myself. Shouldn't have given him that.

I open both eyes and sit up straight. A five hour bus ride is sure to fuck your back right over.

"Where did you get this?" The sound of his voice grates on me.

"What?" I say, barely hiding my irritation, and he shows me what he's fiddling with. A six inch blade flashes in the scarce light. I grab his arm furiously.

"What the hell are you doing?" I hiss through my clenched teeth.

He smiles calmly.

"It was sticking out of your bag, man, just wanted to have a look."

"Give it to me," I say.

For some reason he hesitates. I repeat my words in syllables. He hands me back my hunting knife. I look at him, despising everything about him. The psycho; what was he doing rummaging through my bag?

"It's for hunting," I say and slide it into its sheath.

"Ah yes, thought you were a sportsman. What's your biggest kill?" He asks. "I don't know," I say. "A moose? A bear?" He slides up close to me, whispering in my ear, "A person?"

My patience is running thin. I turn around so I'm facing the guy, our noses only inches away from touching. He doesn't flinch. Instead he just stares into my eyes as if my face was a mirror.

"I don't know who you think you are or what kind of game you're playing," I say as calmly as I can manage, "but I want nothing to do with it."

"I'm not playing any games. I go hunting all the time," he says, and then adds in sort of a whisper; "but don't you ever wonder what it would be like?"

"What would what be like?" I ask without wanting to know the answer. "You know, killing someone."

"No."

"Come on, everyone does."

"Do you?"

"All the time."

I look at him, "You're a freak," I say, hating myself for even engaging with this punk. He looks unfazed by my accusation.

"Come on, man," he says, "Animals kill. A lion wouldn't think twice about ripping the throat out of another lion. It's nature. That's where it's at."

I just shake my head, but he leans towards me over the armrest, relentless in his pursuit of getting me to admit to a truth that he's fabricated in his own mind.

"What would you have done if I was that Lee guy? Think you would have had the guts to defend yourself?"

For a moment I don't know what to say. I can't quite read his face; his features look almost sculpted on, and for a moment I'm not even sure if he's really human. He looks more like a puppet, or someone in a bad disguise. I decide I'm gonna beat him at his own game.

"Maybe I would," I say.

"Yeah?"

I look at the blade in my hands, slowly turning it. I picture it all in my head.

"It wouldn't be much different from finishing off a deer, I suppose".

He scoffs at this, "you're full of it, kid. I saw you sitting there when you thought I was sleeping. Panicking, thinking you were going to die. I bet I could take that knife back right now and you wouldn't do a thing to stop me."

"You're fucking insane," I say.

"And you're a pussy," he says. "You carry a big knife around, thinking you're the boss, but you're afraid of using it."

"Shut your damn mouth," I say. I clench the handle of the knife, infuriated.

He shows his teeth in his fake, plaster grin, opening his arms as if welcoming me.

"Stab me. Come on, stab me," he says.

Yet, as I grab his hair I can't help but detect a touch of resistance. At this point it's too late, though, my knife is already at his throat. The blade slices through his flesh like play dough. A smiling gash opens in his neck and a flood of red M&Ms gushes onto my lap and my seat.

I grab his hair even tighter and start to saw at his throat. It's hard work, but I'm determined now, blindly slashing at his neck. I stop for a second to catch my breath; his head is now only attached by a strip of skin. It snaps like a rubber band at the edge of my knife. There is a gurgling sound like the last bit of water escaping through a drain. Finally his body falls back in the seat while I'm still holding on to the head. A last red M&M pops out of a severed tube in his neck and hits me right between the eyes.

I sit back with his head in my lap. Like this his face looks pale and soft like marzipan; I can shape it to anything I like. My knife is still sharp and cuts easily through the cartilage of his nose. I take an ear as well, putting both in my pocket, just in case.

I start to realise the bus has come to a halt and everything has gone quiet. I'm sitting in my seat, counting the blue dots of the pattern in the plush. Outside a dog is barking. Then, I hear the doors swing open in the front and someone slowly ascending the stairs. They come walking down the aisle. There's the sound of a gun being loaded; a shaky voice tells me to lie down on the floor. I do as I'm told and lay down next to my seatmate's feet. His head is smiling at me from underneath the seat across. Somewhere someone is throwing up.

"Well, he told me to do it," I tell them.

As they pull me away these are the words I keep repeating: "He told me to do it. He told me to do it."

Lego Sword

ALEXANDRA DAVIS

there's an engine running and I
can't stop it always twitching
fiddling my mum says and so
I keep building building anything
really like this lego sword you
don't think of lego being life-
size and long or actually useful
but I can hold this and wield this
and I've put blue glass studs on
the hilt to make it beautiful like
a real sword because inside I am
a real knight but outside I am just
fake but I'm sort of pleased with
this lego sword blocks of grey on
grey see how sharp corners can
become smooth even special like
an emblem of honour or horror
of duty or death which I think
about not just in history lessons
anyway my mum says I make
everything into a weapon even
a barbie doll once but now I've
made this lego sword I want to
hold it always even in bed but
I must lay it down before I fall
asleep so I don't crush it by
rolling on it in the night and
destroying it because it is
so fragile and in pieces
it has painful edges
and would be
torture to
lie on
top
of

Nyctophilia

JENNIFER GLEDHILL

(N) Love of darkness or night; finding relaxation or comfort in the darkness

IN CHINA, DURING the reign of Hizen-Feng, the concubines of the two previous emperors kept silk moths as pets. They liked to watch the moths mating. The game was to tear the moths apart as they were copulating and watch them bleed to death. They lived in the Palace of Benevolent Tranquillity. That image comes to me every night as I sit out on the terrace, looking down at the sunken garden, as the moths flutter by attracted by the lights and the strongly scented plants.

I wonder if that is what they had in mind when they planted this garden and chose only plants that are attractive at night. Scented plants whose fragrance is strongest and most delectable in the darkness like the Night Philox 'midnight candy' *(Zaluzianskya Capensis),* whose scent of honey, almonds and vanilla drifts on the breeze. When planting a night garden due care has to be taken not to pick scents that will overwhelm and clash. Flowers with light colours that reflect the moonlight. Moonflowers (*Datura Meteloides*), they open in the evening, closing their white petals when the sun rises and touches them. White Tussock (*Nassella Tenuissima*), a delicate, fine textured ornamental grass with silky thread-like leaves and flowers that shimmer silver in the moonlight.

A night garden's beauty comes from not just finding flowers

that open at night or are fragrant in the dark but by finding plants that create interesting shadows in the early evening and later in the darkness. I studied the History of Gardens at University.

The scent from the plants mingles with the fragrance coming from my China rose tea. My sister bought it for me one day in Betty's. She thought I might find it soothing. I had not seen her for the longest time before that. We had fallen out and she had not been speaking to me. She rang and said she wanted it to be over. That she missed me.

I shuffle the polaroids in my hand like a deck of tarot cards. Old memories. I spread the polaroids out and rearrange them back into date order. Six in total. I set them out. In two rows of three like a collection of butterflies pinned down in a display. Do they kill them first? Or just pin them down with needles while the butterfly still tries to beat its wings to escape? Of course I know; you told me. *Killing jars sometimes damage the butterflies' wings; they panic and batter their wings against the sides. A better way is to kill them by hand, squeezing the thorax; it's a hard technique to get right so you have to practice on a few common moths first. Ones you are not planning to add to your collection.* You used to put them into frames, all neatly labelled, and display them behind your desk.

I moved into the house two weeks ago; there are still boxes waiting to be unpacked. I'm considering giving them away without opening them and starting again. I should have done it today but instead I fell asleep in the midmorning and woke before evening. "Won't you be lonely though, Rowan?" Maria, my girlfriend asked doubtfully when I told her I was moving out.

There is an unspoken question about how I have afforded the house. I tell other people I'm a professional gambler. I told Maria that I wanted to move back home to be closer to my family. She pretended to believe me but she would watch me out of the corner of her eye. When we first got together she used to ask me "Rowan, what are you plotting now?" I loved the way she used to say my name.

I liked the idea of a house when I first thought about it

but now I'm not so sure. Houses get filled with memories; they sink in through the plaster. You have to fill them with objects. Trinkets from holidays abroad. Shops have started to sell faux Victorian objects. Big glass cloches that belong in a lush hothouse or with little arrangements underneath them in a drawing room. Pictures with painted butterflies on in dark heritage colours. I looked for a long time at the globes. I spun one; idly I watched the tiny islands going round.

Simonides, the poet, used objects as a way to remember. He created memory palaces. You create a path in your mind of a room in your house that you know well and then assign things you want to remember to different objects within that room. Gamblers use a small circular garden instead of a house. The ever-changing randomness of the growing plants is meant to help them deal with the changing patterns and fortunes. It is meant to resemble a roulette wheel. I confess to never understanding that properly and suspecting that someone made it up. Do you think that you could use it to forget? I could leave the memories buried here. One of my last memories of you is when I was ten. My sister, Bracken would turn fourteen soon and my mother would decide that she was old enough to watch me during the summer holidays. You and mum broke up. I never knew why exactly. Mum said you had moved away for work.

My hatred of you was instinctive. It was primordial. I watched you through half closed eyes. If I was a cat, I would have been hissing and spitting, tail shaking, ready to pounce to defend my patch of hot sunlight. My body vibrated with it. My mother had made me come spend time with you. She could sense my dislike. I burned with it. The two of you were thinking of getting married and she thought she could mould us into one happy family. Bracken wasn't made to come. She was always better at hiding her emotions than me. I seethed with mine. We were in your garage. You had the garage door open to let in the air. The sun shone in my eyes, blinding me. I moved into the shadows at the edge where the light didn't reach me.

You were a Lepidopterist. Your ex-wife had made you keep

the paraphernalia connected to your hobby out here. She couldn't stand the thought of it being in the house and, even though, she had taken the children and left you some years ago, you never moved the stuff inside. You told me all this while you went about your business. In the corner was a freezer where you kept the butterflies that you had caught. *They have to be put in the freezer to kill off any parasites, otherwise they might destroy them.* In my mind you kept the freezer drawers carelessly filled with the bodies of butterflies, tumbling on top of each other and covered in ice. I should have known that you were much too meticulous to allow that kind of disorder. My eyes followed you as you walked over to the freezer. I held my breath as you opened the door and pulled open one of the drawers. Inside were clear plastic boxes neatly stacked one on top of each other. As you picked up one of the boxes, you dislodged something hidden in the back behind the boxes. I moved nearer to get a better look. It was the first time I had ever voluntarily come near you. I saw something all bound together with a rubber band. Playing cards? I thought, confused; why were you keeping a deck of cards in your freezer? In a quick motion you moved to block my view and tucked what I thought were playing cards back out of sight and slammed the door.

The butterflies that you had just gotten out needed to defrost before you could do anything with them, but you had got some other ones out earlier to show me what to do. You patiently explained what you were doing, talking more to yourself than to me. *If you can try to collect two of the same specimen then you can show the underside of the wings.* You carefully labelled them, writing the labels out in fountain pen, in an even copperplate, on slips of paper. The name of each insect, sex, age, date and place they were caught. You displayed them in groups by family. Two of each; one male, one female. High Brow Fritillary *(Argynnis Adippe),* family: Nymphalidae, Marsh Fritillary *(Euphydryas Aurinia),* Family: Nymphalidae. Large Cooper *(Lycaena Dispar),* Family: Lycaenidae, Large Blue *(Masculinea Arion),* Family: Lycaenidae. Swallowtail *(Papilio Machaon),* Family: Papillonidae. The Nymphalidaes were your favourites. When you were finished you closed the garage door leaving us hidden from view. *See there is nothing to be afraid of.*

Two white butterflies flew past me. It looked like they were dancing. I hoped that you would leave them alone. They were just Small White (*Pieris Rapae*), too common to be of interest to you. Bracken and I had got tired and fed up walking in the woods. You told us to wait in the clearing for you. It was one of the hottest days of summer. We had been bickering with each other as we trailed after you in the heat. This would be the first time I tried to talk to her about what you had done to us. What you were still doing to me. I was kicking at the sandy soil at the roots of the tree.

"Bracken" I said quietly dropping our argument, tears ran down my face. "Do you remember when I was little and.... made us ... and he used to make you... " I could never say your name. Bracken cut me off the way she would whenever I tried to talk to her about it over the years. The last time she would stop speaking to me for three years.

"Shut up!" She said, "Shut up! Rowan. I never did... there's no way... you couldn't remember that far back".

Is that what you told her to get her to do it? That I was too little? That I wouldn't be able to remember it? She must have known it was a lie. Or did you tell her that you would hurt me worse if she didn't take part? Bracken would have believed that. She already knew how much you had hurt her.

"Brac... Brac...ken I can re...mem...ber," I struggled to get the words out as I gasped for air.

Bracken left me. She walked off back towards the car. I carried on kicking the roots of the tree while I waited for you. You weren't long. I felt your presence behind me before I saw you.

It was two hours later when we returned to the car and found Bracken waiting for you. I followed behind you, stumbling like a sleepwalker. Bracken wouldn't meet my eyes. They were sore and red from crying. You bought me a lolly from the ice cream van. You told me that I deserved it for being a good girl and doing what I was told. You held it out to me. I didn't want it. It made me start crying again. Bracken tried to hold my hand. I flinched from her touch. I licked the lolly in the back of the car as I leaned my head against the window and watched the traffic. I still remember the taste of it. The way the citrus flavour hit the back of my glands making me screw up my face with the tang of it. The way it quenched my thirst and eased my sore throat. I offered it to Bracken. A peace offering. You hadn't bought one for her. She hadn't been a good girl.

I looked out from underneath the bed; my view was blocked by the white swirls of the bed end. I tried to watch the door but the sun was in my eyes making me see patterns and colours. The sun on the window reflected the shape of them on the floor. I wanted to move so that I was better hidden further under the bed. I felt sick and dizzy with the heat. My Mother's room was always the hottest in the house. It was airless today. She had left the window closed. I tried to turn my head to the other side to get it out of my eyes, resting my head on my folded arms. The heat of the sun burned the back of my neck. I felt like my insides were cooking. I turned back to face the door.

Out of the corner of my eye I saw a caterpillar crawling slowly across the floor over the patches of sunlight. It reminded me of the caterpillar from *Alice in Wonderland*. I was worried; someone should have found me by now. I was not well hidden. I watched the door handle move. It was ghostly, even though I knew that it was just someone on the other side. My heartbeat made my whole body pound with the same rhythm. The door opened and I saw white bare feet walking towards me with red painted nails. Bracken. I watched her bare legs walk round to other side of the bed. She opened the window and paused briefly to look out. Bracken turned round to face the bed. I saw her painted toes again. She watched the caterpillar making its slow crawl across the floor. Bracken lifted her bare foot up and brought it down onto the caterpillar, crushing it in between her toes. Bracken smeared its remains across the wooden floor. She left as quietly as she had come in. I often wondered after if you had sent her up on purpose, knowing that she would pretend not to be able to find me, knowing that if she could spare me that, she would. That she would try to protect me. It was late afternoon when I woke up. My mother found me. She was searching one last time before she rang the police. I was known for hiding which was why they hadn't been too worried at first. My sister had sworn she had checked my mother's bedroom. She was such a truthful, reliable girl normally that no-one had thought to doubt her word. There was shouting and she cried. *See, there's no point hiding, you just get your sister into trouble and no-one will believe you if you tell.*

My phone rings; the ringtone reminds me of you. It is what I have been waiting for sitting in the half-light before dawn; the sky is a pale lilac colour. I check the caller ID. It's my mother.

"Rowan..." She's crying; her words are indistinct, "he's dead... Rowan... no-one had seen him... he hung himself".

I wonder who finally found you. Who cared enough about you to check on you? The last time I saw you, you were dangling from the end of a noose in your garage. I was fascinated by the way your smart, black dress shoes swayed slightly. I had come to retrieve something from you. I was surprised that you had left the garage door open.

I hang up on my mother and switch the phone to silent. Later I will tell her that I dropped the phone when my sleeping tablets started to work. She won't believe me. She knows I don't take the tablets. That I had them stock piled in the medicine cabinet in the flat Maria and I shared. Mum found out when Bracken used them to try to kill herself. She stole them from me when she dropped me back at home after we had spent the day together in York. She came in just for a minute to use the bathroom. I threw the rest of them away after that. Bracken's husband rang me a few times afterwards.

"Why did she do it? Did she seem different to you?" he whispered so that she couldn't hear him in the next room.

In the background I could hear the voices of their daughters.

"There were no signs; she's always so happy."

He's scared she'll do it again. What should I tell him? I'd not been close to Bracken for years. Not until that last time at Betty's. And all the time you were insinuating your way back in.

I didn't know you were back until I came back to visit Bracken at the hospital. I had not been back since I left for university. Bracken hadn't told me when she came to see me. Bracken refused to speak to me. She wouldn't even look at me.

I waited outside Bracken's room for Mum. I had come early to the hospital to see Bracken hoping to avoid anyone else. Mum was there though and she made me promise that I would go back with her for a visit. She had something to tell me.

We walked in through the kitchen door. You had your back to us, making tea, looking like you belonged there. Mum told me all about it as we sat around the kitchen table. That you had moved back to the area because of business. Yes, you were back in the same house. No, you'd never sold it. Just rented it out. I heard Maria's voice on the wind, "Rowan, what are you plotting now?"

I loved her for the way she said my name. I sat there across the table from you. Over the years I've learned how to keep a poker face. The memory of the polaroids you had taken of me and Bracken had haunted me all these years. What had you done with them? Kept them, or were they being traded like the way you traded rare butterflies with other collectors?

I broke into your garage that very night, waiting for the early hours when all is quiet and still. Inside I felt the same fear I had always felt. I still imagined that the butterflies were loose in the freezer, their bodies crisp and hard with the ice. I shone the torch on the freezer. It was in the same place where it had always been. You always were a creature of habit. I opened the freezer door and crouched down in front of it. I rummaged through the top drawer where I had seen you try to hide them all those years ago. It didn't take me long to find them hidden behind the boxes of butterflies. I sat back on my heels and took off the rubber band that held them together. I flicked through the photos quickly, trying not to dwell on the images, until I found the one I wanted. It was easy; you kept them all neatly filed in date order. It was one of me from when I was four. I left it on your workbench like a calling card.

It was a week before I rang you to arrange a meeting to tell you my demands. I used my mother's phone. Your relief when you thought there might be a way out. The hope that I would keep my word and not expose you, just take the money and run. Was there ever really a moment where you thought it would be enough? That money was all I really wanted? That I would just leave? Or was it just hope? When it dawned on you that it was not going to happen, how did you feel? I try to picture your face. I would have liked to have seen it. The sense of defeat in your voice when I told you that I was going to take the photographs to the police.

Did you think that even your death would make me hold back at the end? Is that why you did it? I do think about it, just for a moment, as I look at the candle slowly burning out; I think about feeding the photographs to its fading light. I could sell the house and use the money to go travelling. I have such an urge to see the ocean, to feel warm salt water run down my back and to walk on sandy beaches. I could sort it out with Maria, see if she would come with me. Leave it all behind; wash up on some distant shore, re-born by the tides. We could walk together on the beach, hand in hand.

I look at the polaroids on the table in front of me one last time. When I went to your garage to get them I wasn't sure that you would have kept them. The ones of Bracken sickened me the most, even more than the ones of myself. I burned them because I couldn't bear to look at them. The things you made her do. All there, neatly labelled and categorised over the years, in the same copperplate handwriting: sex, age, date and place. It was like you collected your own evidence for me to use against you. I do think about destroying them for good. Maybe if Maria won't come away with me then Bracken would, just for a holiday. I could wait until after your funeral and then ask her. We could go wherever she wanted. We could sit on the beach and read magazines and she could tell me about her children. I would tell her about Maria, about how much I loved her and how my heart was broken. Bracken would give me advice. And Bracken would know that I forgive her. I imagine a nicer life myself. A fresh start by the sea. But I can only ever see it in darkness and for me the sea will always be black and the only sky I can see is the night sky.

The candle has burned itself out. It's morning. I get up and stretch. I'm stiff with being out in the cool air. The Moonflowers are closing as the light starts to touch their petals. Time to go inside and sleep. There is one last, lonely, moth hovering around the light by the door; they evolved to avoid predators.

Coping Mechanism

TRACY FELLS

MY REPLACEMENT IS early. She strides past the kitchen window, tall and willow thin, head erect, taking the path around the side of the house to the back door as if she owns the place. Why doesn't she come to the front and ring the bell like anyone else? Finn mews like a kitten from his moses basket on the floor. He's hungry, needing yet another feed, and the mewing will soon elevate to a piercing wail if I don't pick him up. But I don't want to breast-feed in front of her. I want to brew proper coffee, not flick on the kettle. I want to settle calmly at the oak table and pull out a tin of flapjacks, freshly baked that morning especially for our new houseguest. Milk is leaking through my T-shirt. I'm going to greet the au pair with damp circles around my nipples.

I call her a girl because she's ten years younger than me, recently graduated and starting her life. I call her my replacement because that's the intention: to replace the incompetent mother who can't even satisfy her baby's hunger. Finn fed less than an hour ago; I haven't had time to shower or stack the dishwasher or start a multitude of tasks I won't finish and he's hungry again.

"Hello, Mrs Cave?" The girl calls out as the back door opens inwards. She doesn't knock, just walks straight in.

Our name is Cavell, but I don't correct her.

"Hello, Agnes," I say folding my arms across soggy breasts. "Please call me Hannah."

Thankfully Finn falls silent, giant blue eyes gaping up at her.

"Hannah," says the au pair, her mouth exaggerating the 'H'. "And this must be Finn." Her accent is Eastern European. Cruelly,

I think of those feeble Hammer Horrors set in dark Transylvanian villages. Agnes smiles down at my son. "Can I hold him?"

She peels off knee high black boots, bringing her down to my height. We look each other in the eye. Hers match mine, slate-grey flecked with blue. Almost white lashes and pale skin contrasts against her flushed red lips. Agnes doesn't smile at me. Swinging off her rucksack, her only luggage, she then swoops down to gather up Finn. He gurgles, a rare signal of contentment, and plump fingers reach for Agnes's long blond hair draping her shoulders like silk.

"Be careful," I warn. "It will really hurt if he starts tugging."

"Is no worry." Agnes bounces Finn in her arms. "He is strong little boy. Little man," she coos and kisses his nose.

"Coffee?" I scuttle to the sink. Fill the kettle. Drag an opened packet of Hobnobs down from the cupboard, my earlier breakfast. She should be doing this, I realise, making me coffee. Steven has brought Agnes into our home to look after me.

"I should do this," says Agnes.

She hands Finn to me, then takes two mugs from the cupboard next to the Aga I never use. How does this girl know my kitchen?

"Steven show me all around."

I don't like how my husband's name sounds on her lips.

Steven, along with his mother, had called in and interviewed four candidates for the position of our au pair. This was the day after Finn rolled off his changing mat on the sofa when I left him, only for a second, to answer the phone. I didn't know babies could roll at that age. He didn't hurt himself, but that wasn't the point as Steven and his mother continued to point out.

"Agnes was by far the most suitable," he told me during a stilted Sunday lunch at his parents. I couldn't be trusted with cooking either.

"She spoke the best English," his mother chipped in, "and seems bright enough to cope with Finn."

Mother and son bowed their heads in unison, returning to plates of roast beef and Yorkshire puddings pooled with gravy. Their unspoken accusations congealed, conspiring with the potatoes, cold and untouched at the centre of my plate. Because I couldn't cope with Finn. Couldn't cope with keeping my son or myself fed, clean and happy. An au pair was their perfect solution for coping with me.

Finn fidgets, fights against my cuddle. His cheeks redden as he begins to cry again.

"He needs feeding," I tell Agnes.

She picks up her rucksack, tosses back her hair.

"Is no problem. I will go to my room." The replacement glances around my kitchen. "Then I clean up and make us lunch."

"Shall I show you to your room?"

Agnes shakes her head. There is still no smile for me.

"Steven show me."

Of course he did.

"Do you think she looks like me?"

Steven doesn't look up from his iPad, flicks a finger across the screen.

"I guess. But I didn't know you then."

"What do you mean?" I turn on my side, watch my handsome husband as he continues to work in bed, another once strictly upheld rule overthrown by parenthood. Once upon a time our marital bed was for sex and sleep, in that order.

He taps his bare chest idly.

"You know, when you were at college."

"You mean when I was younger – when I was her age." I slump back against the pillow. The clean T-shirt I'd put on for bed was already blotched with a milk stain. "I felt a right dairy cow when she arrived this morning. Stood there, massive udders squirting, no make-up and Finn on the floor like a workhouse baby, while she swans in, fairy tale gorgeous, swishing her hair like Rapunzel."

Steven carefully places the iPad on his bedside table.

"Why was Finn on the floor?"

I sigh, close my eyes before answering.

"Finn was in his basket. The one your mother gave us, which I can carry from room to room so I never have to leave him alone."

He nods, rubs the black stubble dotting his chin.

"She does look a bit like Rapunzel. Did you notice it goes

all the way down to her bum?" Steven slips down under the duvet, pushes away a loose strand of hair to kiss my cheek. "You could grow your hair long again, I'd like that."

At six months I'd cut my hair to shoulder-length; everyone said it would be more manageable when the baby came. At eight months I took it even shorter to a box cut bob, sleek and stylish. Steven said he loved the new look. Called me a 'Yummy Mummy'. Now I knew how he really felt.

His hand is snaking up inside my T-shirt.

"I also like these massive tits."

I'm trying not to let him see the tears. He hates it when I cry. Turning away I feel him press into my back. His hardness was all it used to take.

"Sorry," I mumble. "I'm still sore down there." Like most natural deliveries I'd been cut to ease Finn's escape.

Steven withdraws his hand. He lies back and I hear him pick up the iPad.

"Okay," he says quietly.

As I finally slip into sleep Finn wakes in the nursery. Despite hugging the pillow close to my ears I still hear his cries through the wall. I recognise the distinctive demand for food. He's hungry again. My body tenses waiting for the click of Agnes's door. Surely she will go to him?

Steven is sprawled across most of the bed, squeezing me to the very edge. Black lashes twitch as he dreams. Finn's cries loop into a continuous screech. Clearly Agnes, like Steven, can sleep undisturbed through Finn's vocal assaults, as there's no sign of any movement from her room.

"You're his mother," Steven had said to me when we first came home from the hospital. "You're tuned to his frequency."

Slipping out from my warm cocoon under the duvet I shiver as the cool night air slaps me fully awake. Finn's screams shake the house. Only the dead could sleep through this. Steven brushes a finger under his nose but doesn't wake. My husband and our new au pair are clearly in league with the dead.

Over the following weeks I fall into a routine with Agnes. I become Finn's wet nurse. Feed on demand, then rest and barely eat in between. Agnes tackles everything else: changing and bathing Finn, cleaning the house, shopping, sorting Steven's dry cleaning (two suits a week) and all the cooking. She sings as she works, melodies I don't recognise and words I can't understand.

"Romanian folk songs," she tells me. "My grandmother taught me."

My guess at Transylvania was close.

One afternoon I'm curled on the sofa drifting in and out of sleep. Finn is feeding every two hours now without fail. Exhausting, but at least he's settled into a predictable pattern. With the TV chattering in the background I dream of Helen, my elder twin and spitting image. She's trying on my favourite white skinny jeans, spinning round to admire her perfect bottom in the full-length mirror of our bedroom. I swear she's wearing my Jimmy Choo heels, the crimson pair Steven bought me after the first positive pregnancy test. Her long fingers twist a necklace around her neck, pale pink pearls like the ones I wear for Steven when I want to have sex. I'm usually naked when I wear those pearls.

The dream is a lie. I can no longer squash my flabby baby belly into those jeans and they wouldn't fit Helen either. Helen died in a car accident when we were ten.

Something touches my shoulder. I smell coconut, the synthetic tang of manufactured sweetness. Agnes leans over me, long hair tickling my cheek. The coconut scent is shampoo, is she using mine? I'll check her bathroom tomorrow when she takes Finn out in his buggy. She springs back as I sit up quickly, swinging my legs off the sofa.

"You have tattoo," says Agnes.

I pull my T-shirt back in place to cover the fraying bra-strap.

"Yes, I've had it since I was a teenager."

"Just one?"

"Yes." Instinctively, I reach to scratch my left shoulder. I can't feel the tattoo, but this action is always comforting.

"And Steven does not mind?"

Agnes is wearing a pair of white jeans, clinging like a second skin to her slim legs.

"No," I answer, but then hesitate. This girl works for me. I should tell her to mind her own business. "Steven loves it."

"What is in bird's mouth?"

I'm eye level with her crotch. Staring at the white skinny jeans. Is she wearing my clothes? I wonder how to pose this question.

"The bird – it's a dove. In its beak is the letter 'H'." The dove is painted with white ink, the letter blood red. I chicken out and say, "I have the same pair of jeans."

"'H' for Hannah?"

Helen had always been the better dancer. She'd been picked to dance the Sugar Plum Fairy in our ballet school's Christmas performance of *The Nutcracker*. I'd sulked at home with Auntie Rachel, pretending I had a tummy ache so I didn't have to watch my sister prance about in her tutu, hand-stitched with silver sequins that sparkled like diamonds. I wasn't in the car when the lorry hit Dad's BMW head on. Wasn't there when the fire took hold, trapping Mum and Helen.

But I'm not going to tell her any of this.

"Yes, the H is for Hannah."

Standing I expect Agnes to step out of my way, but she is so close I can feel her breath. She must have switched the TV off while I slept. The house is quiet. Eerily quiet. I realise why.

"Where's Finn?" There's a tremor of panic in my voice.

Agnes rolls her eyes towards the ceiling. "He sleeping upstairs."

On cue the silence ends with Finn's sharp cry. Two hours to the minute from his last feed. I sigh.

"He was sleeping."

Agnes shrugs. "He is hungry."

He's always fucking hungry I want to scream in her face. I could ask her to move. Tell her to fetch Finn. Give her an order and expect instant obedience. Her grey eyes watch me for a moment. She sinks onto the sofa, picks up a magazine from the coffee table.

Breathing heavily I step over her legs. After feeding Finn I'm going to check the wardrobe, dig out my white jeans. With the constant milk production I must be losing weight. Maybe I can fit into them again.

Finn turns his head, spits out my nipple. Stubby fingers push my breast away as he screws up his eyes and screeches his frustration.

Turning him round I try the other breast and he latches on like a lamprey. The sucking reflex is immediate; his lips tug and tug pulling me further and further away from myself. Nails scratch the dimpled skin around my nipple as he rages against the slow supply. This mother-baby nursing experience is supposed to calm us, bond us close, but Finn hasn't read the baby books. This is his battlefield. After several minutes he's drained me dry and wriggles to get free. I see us in the bedroom mirror. A pink-faced baby squirms in the white arms of a boney wraith. My hair is dull and tangled, eyes aching. I'm a nightmare hag skulking in the shadows, about to steal back the changeling baby.

In the kitchen Agnes is talking on our telephone. Twisting a strand of golden hair she laughs, a low, deep laugh from the back of her throat. Finn is quiet, sucking on my finger. This has appeased his anger but I doubt it will keep him happy for long. He could be teething and not hungry for once.

Steven's mother believes I pander to Finn.

"He's just teething, Hannah. Rub a little brandy into his gums. That always worked for Steven," she shared at her last visit. "Have you tried Calpol?"

"He's too young for Calpol," I replied, glancing to Steven. But he and his father were heads down at the kitchen table, immersed in the Sunday supplements. The men have evolved their own coping mechanisms.

"Nonsense." Steven's mother snorted. She started searching through the cupboards, tutting each time the contents displayed my failings. "I'll pick you up a bottle from the chemist's next time I come over."

Agnes sees me, but continues her conversation. Several weeks under our roof and her accent is fading fast, she's starting to sound like me, a middle-class suburban housewife. In profile I imagine this is how my younger self once looked. Shining eyes. Open lips flushed and ready to devour everything life has to offer. The symmetry of her bone structure is familiar. She could be me. An odd thought makes me shiver. She could be Helen. This is exactly how Helen would look at twenty-two.

Agnes blinks slowly, looks directly at me.

"She's here now. Do you want to speak to her?" Agnes holds

out the telephone. "It's Steven," she says. Not *your* husband or even Mr Cavell, but Steven.

I snatch the phone. Before I can say anything he's gushing on about some deal he's pulled off. We need to celebrate so he's invited his parents over for dinner on Saturday night. He's giving me plenty of warning; Saturday is three whole days away, so I have time to sort out a menu for Agnes to prepare. Plenty of bubbly – the deal is a big one – we don't need to scrimp so I can get the proper stuff, not a supermarket brand. Scurrying to the lounge, the phone propped on my shoulder and Finn still in my arms, I tell him Agnes is a thief.

"Don't be an idiot, Hannah," says Steven, "of course she hasn't taken your jeans. She's just got a similar pair."

I hiss into the phone, "How could she afford the same ones? I looked in the wardrobe – they're not there! I'm sure other stuff is missing too. That cream top you like, with the diamante straps. My furry ankle boots."

"Hannah." He's using the same tone he reserves for Finn and little dogs, mock cutesy. "Have you looked everywhere? In the washing basket?"

For a pair of ankle boots? I want to shout back. Instead I drop my voice to a whisper.

"Yes, of course I have."

"If you find the top can you wear it on Saturday? It looks great with your pink pearls."

I end the call so he can't tell I'm crying. Even if I do find his favourite top it no longer fits over my double 'D' milk factories. But it would look fantastic on Agnes, along with the pearls.

Agnes is still in the kitchen; I can hear her slicing veg for dinner. Finn is asleep, but to put him down could break the spell so I hold his head above my heart, then I tiptoe upstairs to check my jewellery box.

Steven stands behind me as I brush my teeth. He throws something to the floor.

"Bloody hell, Hannah, what's going on inside your head? These were at the bottom of the washing basket."

White skinny jeans lie crookedly, like broken legs, beside my bare feet. I don't say anything. I'm naked wearing only a string of pink pearls.

"You look exhausted," he continues more gently. "Are you getting enough rest during the day? You should use Agnes to do as much as possible. She can look after Finn."

He pinches the flesh under my arm.

"Are you eating enough? You're skin and bones. Christ, Hannah, you need to look after yourself better than this."

Using the back of my hand I wipe toothpaste from my lips.

"But she can't feed him for me. He never stops gorging. He's always hungry, Steven. Always at me." Tears plop into the porcelain sink. "He's a monster."

I expect his anger to deepen, but he strokes the back of my neck.

"Hush, sweetheart. Tomorrow morning I'll make an appointment for you and Finn to see the Health Visitor. Perhaps, there's some sort of problem…"

He means with me. There's a problem with me.

Steven's fingers hesitate over my dove tattoo then linger on the warm pearls; he fumbles with the clasp and slips them off my neck.

"I don't think either of us is really in the mood tonight," he says.

Dr Pearson is called in to see me. The Health Visitor isn't happy with Finn's progress. He's not putting on weight despite the constant feeding and the situation can't be allowed to continue.

"How are you coping, Mrs Cavell?" Dr Pearson smiles like a boy. He barely looks older than Agnes.

I promise myself I am not going to cry, but he's not playing the game by opening with such a question. Looking down at my lap, I shake my head.

"Clearly Finn is running you ragged. It's a vicious circle. He's constantly feeding because he's constantly hungry. You never recover so can't produce enough milk to satisfy him."

Steven and his mother are right. The problem is me.

Dr Pearson explains there is a solution. I could kiss his baby face. I could strip naked and let him take me right there in the surgery because he has an answer. Formula milk will allow me to cope and I can switch Finn immediately. This means somebody else can feed him, even during the night. I can rest, sleep, even leave the house without him. My boobs can return to normal and I can start having sex with my husband again.

This time I'm crying with relief.

I wake at five o'clock having slept through since ten the night before. Seven hours of consecutive sleep! Dr Pearson, along with the manufacturer of formula milk, is a miracle maker. Turning over I stretch out for Steven, but the sheet is cold; he must be up already. I almost hold my breath listening out for Finn's cries, but hear nothing. The creak of the central heating system is the only indication that the house is stirring, preparing for the day ahead.

Steven is in the kitchen making coffee. I slip my arms around his waist, kiss his warm neck. His skin smells shower clean, feels smooth, he must have just shaved.

"You're up early," I murmur and begin to nibble at his earlobe.

He looks at his watch.

"Long day today – gotta close that deal remember. Lots of loose ends to tie up. You sound perky this morning."

I smile lazily.

"I feel great. See, all I needed was a good night's sleep."

"And Finn?"

"What about Finn?"

Steven pulls away from me, pours coffee into his travel mug.

"Have you checked on him?"

"Not yet." My good mood is wilting already. "It's all quiet upstairs so I assume he's still sleeping."

"But you didn't check?" Steven pulls on his jacket, tightens his tie. "He was crying in the night. Did you feed him?"

The tiles under my bare feet feel ice cold.

"No, I slept straight through. Agnes said she would make a bottle if he was hungry."

"So the au pair is now feeding my son?"

"That is one of the benefits of switching to formula," I say, keeping my voice calm.

His shoulders sag.

"So you're sticking with this then? Giving up on the breast feeding for good."

"Finn is always hungry because I'm not producing enough milk. Dr Pearson was worried about Finn's weight, apparently he's dropped under the growth curve." I keep talking because Steven's eyes are staring into me. His jaw is clenched. "Lots of women stop breast feeding a lot earlier than me, it's perfectly normal."

"Did Dr Pearson think your behaviour was *perfectly normal*? Did you tell him about your irrational thoughts, your weird suspicions about Agnes?"

I don't know how to reply. Steven had insisted, demanded, I visit the Health Centre to sort out Finn. Now he was angry with me again, even though I'd done what he'd asked.

Steven's face bounces back into a smile. I reach for his hand, but he's looking past me, into the hallway. Agnes stands at the bottom of the stairs, Finn balanced on one hip gurgling happily. Her lemon silk robe is embroidered with crimson roses; I have one just like it.

She holds out Steven's briefcase, saying without any trace of an accent, "Don't forget this."

I watch my husband stride towards the au pair. He doesn't kiss me goodbye or even look back. For one dreadful moment I think he's going to kiss Agnes, but he leans down to Finn and kisses the top of our baby's head.

I often play a game with myself: imagine what Helen would be doing now if I'd been chosen for *The Nutcracker*. If I'd died with Mum and Dad on the A27 that December afternoon and she'd stayed home, then what sort of life would Helen be living in my place? I doubt her husband would hire an au pair behind her back. Nor would she meekly let a thieving, lying stranger usurp her position. Helen would look for proof and catch the bitch out.

Steven is getting the Champagne I forgot to pick up for tonight's dinner with his parents. He's taken Finn along, for once, and Agnes's joined them as she's booked an appointment with the beauty salon in the village. This means I'm alone in the house. Alone to explore Agnes's room.

I don't find a pair of white jeans in her wardrobe; neither

do I find any of my missing things. The top drawer of her bedside cabinet is full of underwear. The other drawers are empty. So too is the antique dressing table, squatting like a Victorian cuckoo in the small room. Disappointingly there is nothing belonging to me in Agnes's bedroom.

Having been deprived of sleep for so long my body now seeks every opportunity to lie down and sink into oblivion. Pressing my face into the clean white pillows I smell lavender. I smell long hot summer days when Helen and I splashed and giggled in our paddling pool. Dad would fill it on the patio using the hosepipe that leaked from the rusty garden tap. I can just lie down for a moment. Think through all the places Agnes could hide my pearls. Steven won't be back for hours.

When I wake the room is dark. The day has slipped by. It must be early evening. Nobody has come to find me.

In the hallway I hear voices from the dining room. The clink of crystal. The lilting rise and fall of easygoing chatter between dinner guests. Steven's parents must be here already. Oddly, the kitchen is empty. The electric oven is humming and my stomach cramps at the aroma of roasting meat. Steven's probably showing off Agnes to his mother. *This is Hannah's replacement. She cooks and cleans and never drops Finn on his head. Isn't she wonderful!*

The dining room door swings open. Steven's mother carries dishes through to the kitchen with Steven in her wake. She's in full flow.

"The au pair must be doing something right; Helen's looking absolutely marvellous. Such a clever decision of yours, darling, to get some help in."

Why did she call me Helen?

Steven sees me in the doorway. His eyes narrow, the relaxed smile vanishes.

"Where the hell have you been, Agnes?" he says sharply, pausing only to stack the pile of soup bowls he was holding on the draining board. "Helen's had to prepare everything herself."

They're both frowning at me. All I can do is stutter back,

"W-what are you talking about? I'm Hannah."

Steven's mother wipes her hands on a tea towel.

"Then why did you tell my son your name was Agnes?" She

turns to Steven. "I told you to hire an English girl. Did you check her references?"

I have to see for myself.

In the dining room Agnes sits at the head of the table with Finn on her lap. He's beaming like a Buddha, sucking on a breadstick. Her long hair has been cut into a slick short bob. She's wearing my cream top with diamante straps. A pink pearl necklace around her flushed neck.

"I can't believe what you've done to your hair," says Steven.

He knocks my elbow as he strides past to stand behind Agnes. With palms pressed against her arms he looks back at me.

"First you steal Helen's clothes and now you cut off all your hair. This is beyond a joke."

He's shouting at me. Not at Agnes. At me.

The dove tattoo on Agnes's left shoulder is clearly visible in the round mirror behind her. Then I realise I'm looking at her reflection. The tattoo is actually on her right side – the opposite shoulder to mine.

The young woman in my seat stares at me.

"Helen?" I whisper almost hopefully, calling out to the past. Her grey-blue eyes are unreadable. She doesn't smile or acknowledge me in any way.

Steven's mother joins in the shouting. Finn begins to cry. I step forward, to go to my son, but Steven's cold glare fixes me. Agnes whispers something to Finn. He drops the breadstick, whimpers and reaches for her neck.

I back out of the dining room and run to Agnes's bedroom where I trip over her rucksack, the only luggage she brought into our house.

I can cope with this, I chant inside my head. Like I coped with Helen's death. Coped without Mum and Dad.

I start packing clothes into the rucksack. Under a book on the bedside cabinet is a pile of cash – I grab it all. From the ensuite bathroom I take make-up and toiletries, even her toothbrush.

Downstairs Steven and his parents are talking loudly. Finn is no longer crying. With my hand on the door latch I feel a knot of pain in my breast, as if someone is squeezing inside, but my milk dried up days ago. My replacement is coping.

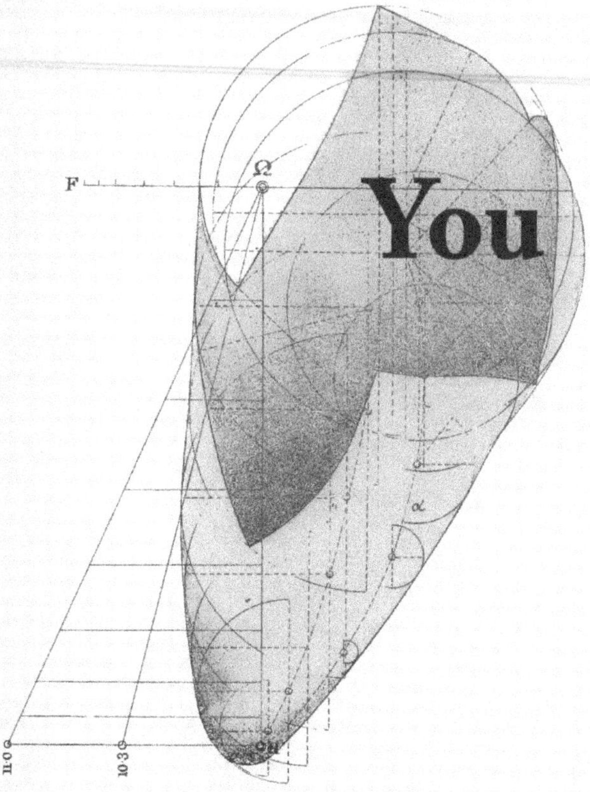
You
F
Ω
α

Running Naked On The Motorway

WES LEE

you didn't dodge the raindrops
the way they say bees do. The rain

pelted hard. You felt every drop –
flashed and honked by truck drivers, men

coming home in cars, but no-one stopped.
A look of abject terror on your face,

determined to get to somewhere safe,
and the man following behind who had taken time

to pull on his trousers.

Space Diving

OLIVIA RANDALL

YOU CLOSE YOUR eyes and you fall. You fall and you fall and you fall upwards and you're soaring and you open your eyes and you're surrounded by pink and purple and stars and infinity. Everything is glimmering. Everything is beautiful. Nothing is wrong.

It's years before you notice you're dead.

Van Gogh ate yellow paint because he thought it would bring him happiness. Yellow is the sun and daffodils and buttercups. It's lemons and canaries and autumn leaves. Yellow is warmth and joy; it's enthusiasm, it's optimism and it's happiness. True happiness. Van Gogh thought that eating yellow, toxic paint would blind the sadness inside him and make him feel happy again. Can you imagine being so empty of joy that you try to fill the void by poisoning yourself? Can you imagine being so desperate to feel happiness again?

There are other, more dangerous ways to try to feel emotions again. You know that. You took a lot of drugs just to get a reaction, but you stopped when you woke up in hospital for the fourth time. You fell in love once or twice, hoping that would fill the void – but it didn't, not really. It just ended with a few heartbreaks and the overwhelming sense that you were lost. You wonder if you're selfish. Do you think that no-one else is lonesome? Do you think that no-one else lives in the abyss? You know that other people have their demons but you also know that no-one will ever, *ever* truly understand.

Maybe you *are* selfish.

You take your tablets four times a day. You cry sometimes. You smoke more and more and more. You consider tripping acid. You consider trying to meet someone new. You think, *everyone has their own version of yellow paint*. You pause. You consider eating yellow paint. Instead, you don't eat anything at all. You lie in bed and feel nothing. You watch *The X-Files*. You ignore the ghosts. You lie in bed and you feel nothing.

At night, your demons crawl out of the shadows. They hiss and grieve and slither into bed with you, wrapping around your body. You lie there, frozen and terrified, until the morning comes and they whisper goodbye.

You live with ghouls and wraiths who pester you to follow them. You pretend you can't hear and you take your tablets four times a day and you cry sometimes. And you consider eating yellow paint. Every day. Every day. Every day. You are always on edge and you bite your fingernails down to nothing.

The demons and ghosts are all you have.

Follow me.

You think, *not today*, and you watch *The X-Files* and you lie in bed and you feel nothing.

Follow me.

You think, *not today*, and you consider tripping acid and you lie in bed and you feel nothing.

Follow me.

You think, *not today*, and you smoke more and more and more and you lie in bed and you feel nothing.

Follow me.

You think, *I am having an existential crisis*. You nod and you walk through the veil. The wraith holds your hand and it feels like sadness and smoke and lost time and you're sick to your stomach.

You are on top of a cliff staring down at a deep, black drop. Everything is glimmering. Everything is beautiful. Everything is wrong.

Follow me, says the wraith, and then it falls and then it's gone.

You consider. You consider going back. Back to what? Back to smoking and crying and *The X-Files*? Nobody is as lonesome as you. Not even the demons are grieving like you. You grieve for your happiness. There are more dangerous ways to try to feel emotions again. Everyone has their own version of yellow paint.

What Is There To Say?

L.F.ROTH

YOU ARE SITTING on one side, your son and daughter on the other. No curtains frame the bed – this is a private room. Your daughter is the one who arrived last: there are no trains at night from where she lives, nor does she have a car. When she pushed the door open, cautiously, your son got up to fetch another chair and she took his. He is now close to the foot of the bed but still has an unobstructed view. The head of the bed is raised at a 45-degree angle.

This is not the picture that you see, of course – yours is more limited. You rarely even look across the bed but have your eyes fixed on your husband.

There has been no change. His skin is pale but no more than before. His eyes are still wide open and unseeing. He doesn't blink. After each breath there is a pause, unvaried in length. The tubes are there, just as before: thin ones that run to his nostrils from behind his ears and are connected to the wall outlet for oxygen via a thicker one curled up peacefully on his chest; a catheter that forms a loop at the side of the bed before it disappears out of view. Hospital corners hold the bedclothes in place.

"Will you be back in the morning?" he had asked when you left in the late afternoon.

You had been, every morning, for the last six days, so there was no need for his question, nor for an answer. You nodded, gave him a hug, making sure you stayed clear of all tubes. You didn't turn around in the doorway. You knew he would go back to watching TV or just rest. At this point you regret that you did not – a minor regret, as regrets go, to be followed, no doubt, by countless others. That must be one of the consequences of death.

For a moment you take your eyes off your husband and peer at your son and daughter, wondering how they will cope.

"He loved you very much," you say, keeping your voice down.

You are embarrassed when you realize that you used the past tense. What if he can hear you?

"Still does, I'm sure," you add, though the idea that he should have strong feelings for others at this stage seems almost absurd. You squeeze his hand; you have been holding it since you sat down. You no longer expect a response and there is none.

"Mum, don't," says your daughter.

"Don't what?" you ask.

"Don't treat us like children."

"I'm not," you say.

"You know you are."

You shrug.

"Well, to me you are."

Your son frowns.

"Stop it. Both of you."

He is right – this is not the time or place – but nonetheless, you are annoyed; you shift a little in your chair in remonstrance. As you do, you notice that the trapezelike handle that used to be above the bed is gone; the pole that holds it has been swung around and is kept flush against the wall. No-one will reach for it, of course. Your husband will not lift himself up or adjust his position ever again. You blink to keep back the tears, for though you knew, it hurts. To calm yourself you fix your gaze on the tubes, grey against the white of the gown. You look intently at the pillow, clean but creased, sporting lines like those in the palm of one's hand, held down by his weight – what little weight there is.

"Did you have supper before you set off?" You steal a glance at your daughter as you ask the question, not quite facing her. She has grown thinner, hasn't she? "You have to eat, no matter what."

"Mum, I'm twenty-eight."

"Still."

"Not again." Your son stands up, catching his chair before it hits the floor. "I have to get some air."

He can open the window, you say, but he is gone.

Your daughter ignores you.

Time moves slowly. Your son returns. He doesn't say where he has been. Other than that there are no interruptions. No nurse peeks in, no doctor, though one must be on call. "It won't be long," was the message you received a little after six o'clock; you had just finished your own supper. You had been surprised: when you left him, he had seemed no weaker than before. It is now nearly one. You have been here for well over five hours, as has your son; your daughter close on three.

"Who brought you?" You had not thought to ask. "Clive, was it?"

"Why Clive? I haven't seen him for years."

"He was nice."

"Mum."

But the point is worth making.

"I know," you say. "I liked him, though. You should have..."

"Mum!"

The interruption comes from both of them this time, like a voice with a built-in echo.

You wonder again how much he can hear, if anything. His eyes reveal nothing, nor does his body stir beyond the slight movement caused by the five or six breaths he takes each minute, so quiet, so calm as to be almost imperceptible. Should you try talking to him? If you did, what could you say? What do night nurses talk about when they watch over a patient?

Perhaps your son's thoughts have gone in the same direction.

"I'd like to be alone with Dad," he says.

"Of course." You try to hide your surprise. "Now?" you ask, in case you have misunderstood him, making assumptions that have nothing to do with his needs.

He nods.

"Not after ..."

"No."

"All right."

You let go of your husband's hand and stand up. For a second or two your head spins. This often happens when you get up quickly, but the dizziness never lasts. Your daughter is on her way out. You follow her.

"Come and get us when you're done," you say, hearing as you utter the words that it is the wrong phrase.

The corridor is empty. At one end, in an alcove, is a table with some chairs. Your daughter is on her way there. When you catch up, she has walked over to a window and has her back to you. You join her. Outside the sky is black – you see no moon, no stars. Below, at street level, there is nobody about; there is no traffic at all.

"Does he just want to be with Dad?" you ask.

"I suppose so. Or talk to him. So?"

"Oh, nothing," you say, but that is not what you think. There must be something troubling him and then, why turn to his father? What good will that do at this time?

You sit down at the table. Your daughter remains by the window. Neither of you speaks, but the result is not a comfortable silence.

"Did you offer to pay for the petrol?" you ask.

"Yes," she says.

And had she? She volunteers nothing, but you decide to let it go. Leave her alone, you caution yourself. She doesn't want to talk.

The minutes drag by. There is a clock in the corridor, but if it had not been for the second hand, you would have thought it had stopped. You watch the minute hand. It moves every thirty seconds, soundlessly, and each time trembles slightly in its new position as if the strain involved in getting there had been nearly unbearable. At some point you nod off. When you come to, there is still no sign of your son. Nor is your daughter there.

At two fifteen the door to your husband's room is pulled open and your son comes out to get you. He appears to have been crying, but you are not sure – he may simply have washed his face to stay awake. You do not ask – this is no time for questions – but return to your seat by the bed. The room seems airless after the corridor, but otherwise nothing has changed. Your husband's breathing is still as regular as before, his eyes equally lifeless. You take his hand, again hold it in yours.

"I tried to find a coffee machine."

It is your daughter's voice – you must have nodded off again. Half asleep, you check your watch and see that it is almost three – at least you are getting through the night. You reproach yourself at the thought. That is not what this is about. But what it is about you do not want to face.

"Was there one?" you ask.

But she had only come across a cafeteria that was closed.

"Too bad," you say. "We could all do with a cup." You regret the inclusion, or exclusion, that the word 'all' implies, but any qualification would make matters worse.

Encouraged, perhaps, by your comment, your daughter searches in her handbag. What she brings out is her mobile phone.

"You can't use that here," you tell her. "There are signs everywhere. You'll have to go outside."

"I'd like to take his picture," she says. "Can I, Mum?"

A picture here? You shake your head. This is not how she will want to remember him. Nor would your husband want her to, of that you are sure. To your surprise, she doesn't argue but puts the phone away.

A little before five o'clock you sense that there is a slight change in your husband's breathing. At first you can't determine what that change is – what little sound he makes has not altered at all – but then you realize that the pause between one breath and the next is longer than it was. You grow tense waiting, so intent on listening that you notice nothing else. This could go on forever, you think, fully aware that each breath could in fact be the last. This one. This one. You count the seconds between breaths. You slow the count down as if that would help keep him alive. One more. One more. And then, although there is no final spasm, no desperate last gasping for air, it is obvious that it is over. There is no sound.

A numbness comes over you. You feel shut off from everything around you, from the room you are in, from your son and daughter, but saying that is wrong: you do not feel. You look at the hand you are holding, but there is no-one, no-one, nothing, there. The truth leaps at you: you will never feel again.

Then someone must have fetched a nurse; it may well have been you. The tubes are gone. There is a doctor in the room – there are procedures that have to be followed.

"You'll want a little time alone with him," the doctor says. "Do you want me to close his eyes?"

"No," you say, "I'll do it."

But even as you do, as you move your hand slowly, gently, over your husband's forehead, past his eyes, and softly touch his lips with the inside of your thumb, you know that the picture you will carry with you, the one that will appear superimposed on every memory – when you glance at the chair that used to be his, or across the table where he used to sit, or at his side of the bed as you pull back the covers – what you will see will be what your eyes, your mind, have focused on all night, his head against the pillow, his face divided by the tubes, his eyes unblinking, staring blindly, seeing nothing. Nothing. That is what will remain with you.

You straighten the sheet across his chest.

"There," you say. "There."

But if the words leave your lips, you are the only one who hears them. No-one else.

Happy Birthday, Pauly!

ANDREW MCDONNELL

YOU ARE THIRTEEN years old today and you can't wake your brother up.

It is the school holidays and you and your little brother Adrian like to watch the girls through the fence playing in their swimming pool.

The girls appeared one day in July and were unaware of the infrequent visitors at the perimeter, peering through the fence. The family had planted leylandii as an attempt to further screen their house from the footpath that ran between the summerhouses.

You have to cycle four miles to get to the house with the swimming pool. You discovered it by chance on Monday, when you had walked back from town with your mother. You are used to these walks. They're not for pleasure or for exercise; they are an economic necessity.

You were loaded down with shopping bags and it was one of those days where the sky is white and the heat squats on you. Adrian was mostly upset by small storm bugs that were clinging to his skin in their dozens, whereas you Paul, being older, felt acute self-awareness, fearful that other boys from school might see you.

After the three of you had crossed the long fly-over, you took the footpath across the fields that led to the village. It was at the first stile that you heard the voices of the girls in the swimming pool behind the fence. You and Adrian were desperately trying to see over the fence. Your mother walked in front, lost in her own thoughts – she's always lost in her thoughts isn't she, Pauly?

You made plans to return the next day. That night in bed, all you could think about was the house and the girls: who can blame you, Pauly? The whole thing is an adventure, right? Village life is dull; it's either the smell of perm lotion from the old ladies who come to have their hair done, or the bollard challenge – how many can you make it across before falling? The other children in your little village are hidden on private tennis courts or on long holidays in countries you can't say, let alone spell. You used to go away, when Dad was alive, to Pontins. There's a lovely photo of you all in the Pontins t-shirts with inflatable crocodiles for the swimming pool. You met a girl there Paul, all the way from Liverpool. Her name was Tessa and she showed you how to hear the sea when you hold a shell up to your ear. In the shop they had one that held a pen and you bought two, one for her and one for you. After the holiday you would take it down from the shelf and listen, imagining Tessa floating in the sea. You wrote letters to each other for a short while until you stopped responding. Her handwriting was always difficult to read.

You made sandwiches that morning, eking out the jam that was left at the bottom of the jar. You spilt a bit and when you came back with your bag there was already a trail of ants journeying past each other. You watched them a while before wiping up the splodge with your finger and dabbing it into your mouth. A little curious thing: you apologised to the ants. Then you loaded comics for reading and dug out a disposable camera left unopened in the bottom of the sideboard. Your mum wasn't up. You made her a coffee and a piece of toast. You took it to her room, do you remember? She was awake but didn't say anything. Her curtains were orange; they seemed to make the room warmer. That morning they hung still. There was no breeze. She lay in her nightie on top of the duvet. You spoke to the tattoo of your names on her right shoulder blade. It shrugged in response.

The girls were there again. You found a spyhole for Adrian who had to watch on tiptoe, and one where you had to stoop a little. Through your tiny apertures, another world presented itself. The three girls were obviously triplets. The three girls sat on sun loungers. The three girls talked about boys at school. They talked about someone called Heath Ledger and how he had 'tragically' died ("Spelt t-r-a-g-a-c-a-l-l-e-y"). Adrian kept notes and you would sometimes summon him back to the spy-hole. The girls wore bikinis and they were pale white. When they swam it was *elegant*, ("that's spelt e-l-l-i-g-e-n-t"). How old were they, Pauly? A few years older than you; it made you sad. How would you even engage in conversation with girls like these? Would they even notice a scruffy boy about to turn thirteen and his epileptic stump of a little brother, who cross fly-overs with frozen food fast defrosting? No, that's why you liked to watch; it made you both feel something, like a voice calling on the summer air, something deeper within you was being awoken and it was both confusing and strangely addictive, but you could only move within its edge lands, along the canals and train lines that skirted the centre of a fast growing city. A voice called them in.

"Girls, come in now, we have to go to town!"

After the house had fallen silent, you and Adrian retired to the remnants of the cricket pavilion and went over what you had seen and heard. Adrian read aloud from the notebook, and you, like some Arctic explorer with the taciturn strength of a leader, stared into the distance as if the landscape was a library in which your thoughts could not only be stored, but also indexed, archived and stamped with approval.

Overhead bulbous clouds raced in, like a quilt being pulled across the closing day. Neither of you had ever seen clouds like these ones. Adrian felt afraid. There was something almost apocalyptic about them ("spelt a-p-o-k-o-l-y-p-t-i-c"). You tried to reassure Adrian that all was A-O-K, but you knew then, didn't you, Pauly? Life is deeper and stranger than you could have ever imagined.

There was a huge thunderstorm in the night.

Today is your birthday; you are thirteen and the world feels still, as if time was still. You went through your routines again, breakfast for Adrian, breakfast for mum: her orange curtains still. She gave you a card with a fiver in it. "Buy a nice cake for later" it said inside. But that's a different kind of later, a later that could be in an entirely different dimension of space and time, as there's only one thing on your mind: to return to the swimming pool and log another day.

More sandwiches, more ants and we're off, Pauly; we're off, aiming at huge puddles which are quickly evaporating. Opening gates, throwing bikes over stiles and then on and on, no time to lose now you're a teenager.

But today, on your birthday, the house is silent. You peer through the holes. It is dark, no lights, no voices or anything. You feel something, a feeling that seems to arrive in our teenage years and dog us throughout our lives. You guess it's called disappointment, but like all things, language is a poor indicator for the experience. You turn to tell Adrian that you should go, that you have a fiver and if spent right there could be cake and coca-cola, (maybe even Doritos), but Adrian is halfway over the fence. Then he's gone; he's dropped down and is running across the lawn. You hide your bikes in the hedgerow and go over as well. You land heavily on your ankle and swear, before hopping to the sun loungers. There is a cover over the pool, but Adrian has worked out the winch and is winding it back.

The water looks unreal, a blue that can only be created by chemicals. There are drowning insects on the surface. A wasp is fighting to swim to the other side; you poke it with a stick, pushing it briefly under the water. It rises again and with the same persistence swims on. What if it gets out? Wasps are aggressive – it might attack you. So you push it under again and again, and each time its fight slows that little bit more until it no longer moves against the surface. There are some weird insects, things with cumbersome bodies and impossible legs. You feel sad for those ones, Pauly; they are not struggling, as if they died upon impact. Your thirteen-year-old face is reflected by the blue and you take a reflection selfie on the disposable;

later you may see the wasp that you drowned just centimetres from your warped face.

The post-storm humidity is stifling. Adrian is shouting to you.

"Look at the size of their sofa Pauly! I should write this down!" but you feel heavy and unhappy.

You lie back on a blue sun-lounger and watch as a small plane shuttles across the sky above you, its engine disturbing the stillness. You pretend to shoot it down. What if it fell, Pauly, just dropped out of the sky? You killed a wasp, so why not a pilot?

A riddle for you:

Q. Why can't you hear Adrian?

A. Because he's gone inside! Ho ho.

They haven't locked the patio doors. Everyone always thinks they have locked patio doors, but often they haven't. It is pretty tricky, Pauly; you have to push up a little arm as far as possible and turn the key at the same time. It is easy to get it wrong. Now Adrian is in there on his own. You call his name at the threshold, but there is no answer. You look around the open plan living room and kitchen. Why not look in the cupboards, Pauly? In you go. They might have left some food. Not this cupboard, it has glasses in it. This one is full of rice, spaghetti and something called 'Organic Pearl Barley'. Ah, look, this cupboard is the winner: Doritos! Why not put the television on and enjoy your birthday? It takes some figuring out, but once you find the remote controls you're away.

There are some cartoons; aren't they funny, Pauly! Adi would like these, so call him; it's his favourite, *Spongebob*, but the chair you are sitting on is breaking and you are sprawling on the floor. Get up boy, quick! Look at what you've done! Oh dear Paul Carter of Mildmay Place! The wooden chair, meant for someone smaller than you is splintered and there is no fixing it now! Your Dorito fingers have smeared the white carpet with orange trails; you rub them but it only spreads the grease. It's time to go, Pauly, time to get out! Adrian must be upstairs; you find him in one of the girls bedrooms. He is asleep on her bed.

"Wake up! Come on, Adi!" but he won't stir; he's had a fit and now he's making some deep groaning noises.

The front door and voices below.

"Come on Adi *please* wake up we've got to go, they're home!" but Adrian isn't coming round is he?

Quick! Hide down the side of the bed.

"Who left the TV on?"

"Who's been eating my Doritos?"

"Who's broken baby Sophie's chair?"

"Why is the door open, Mummy?"

"Did you not lock it?"

"Stupid girls, I asked you if you had locked it and you said yes. Flick, call the police NOW!"

"I can't find the phone mummy!"

"Who's had the phone?"

"I think it's upstairs!"

Here they come up the stairs.

"There's someone sleeping in my bed, Mummy!" says a voice.

Someone is hurtling up the stairs with a *clomp, clomp, clomp* and now advances on the bed, and they're shaking Adrian.

Don't cry, Pauly; you're a big boy now, the big 1-3. Oh dear, Pauly, you're peeing your pants!

Pauly, Pauly Carter, pants wetting disaster!

"Wake up, boy, wake up!"

Someone is shaking Adrian; the bed moves against you.

"He's not sleeping," says the adult voice.

The Imperative Mood

CLAIRE MARTIN

YOU ASK YOURSELF an awful lot of questions.

Get a bit overwhelmed and scale it back, settling on just one question to start with. Decide to take things one step at a time, in bite-sized chunks, so as to absorb it better.

Start at the beginning then, with the big question. Ask the big question.

Ask if this is real.

Ask how is it possible for this to finally fall into your lap, like that, as if by chance. Wonder how long she'd been sitting on it, this information, how long she'd been withholding it.

Abandon that line of inquiry. Realise that it will only lead to bitterness and pain and so let go of it, focusing only on this new revelation, this piece of information that you have, finally, after all this time. Breathe in. Remind yourself that you're an adult, a competent, successful adult, and that thinking petty thoughts about your parent is childish.

Think petty thoughts anyway, but only for a moment or two.

Tell yourself sternly to get over it.

Ask why. Ask yourself why, over and over and over again, staring at that crumpled up piece of paper in your hands. Put it down on the coffee table in front of you and smooth it out, carefully, lovingly. Look at it.

Look at those scribbles, the ink creased by the wrinkles in the paper.

Reach out with one fingertip and touch those little black

marks, wonderingly, almost reverentially, and realise that finally *this* might be able to answer those questions.

Think back to all of those teenage years and the rows and the bad behaviour, the grudge held against the world, always, obstinately, wearing it on your sleeve like a badge of honour, a chip on your shoulder that will never go away.

Think of how hard you worked, feeling you had to prove yourself more than the others, and then how badly you misbehaved, overly sensitive to every hiccup and every slight, undermining all of the time and energy put out. Remember the way your mum's face looked, all mottled and red and angry, when you stumbled home late and slurred something insulting at her. Remember that and look at that little piece of paper that could hold all of the answers.

Ask yourself, harshly, if you'll have the strength and courage to do this.

Ask yourself if it'll be worth it.

Think about that.

Pace back and forth, your feet eating up the space in your apartment.

Think of what she said, when she handed the paper over, those acid words that burn in the back of your mind. Remember the tone and the shape of her mouth as she'd said them, I did this for your good.

Decide that yes, it will be worth it, yes, yes, how could it not be.

Decide to do it.

Decide to do it right now.

Sit down. Stand up.

Look around. Take a step, then stop. Breathe, then don't. Hold your breath. Longer. Hold it still, until there's that feeling in your chest, until you're gulping in your throat, until that obstinate feeling, the need for oxygen, rises like a bubble and pushes into your mouth, then breathe in again and exhale, slowly and thoroughly.

Decide to not do it right this minute. Wait until your heart beat has calmed down.

Make yourself a cup of tea. Drink it standing up at the sink, gulping down the burning liquid until your tongue goes numb and you can't feel anything anymore. Dump it down the sink half-finished.

Sit down. Stand up. Fidget.

Circle around the phone, picking it up then putting it back down. Look at that piece of paper, even though you already know those numbers off by heart.

Pick up the phone.

Lose your bottle and have your fingers punch out a familiar number, squeezing your eyes shut against your cowardice.

Order Chinese, as a bribe or a punishment it is hard to say, spicy black bean beef and noodles, and hang up the phone.

Pace. Then stop. Look around. Then don't.

Pick up the phone again. Dial the number, fingers shaking. Hold your breath. Hold it until the hammering of your heart begins to fill your ears, then let it go. Crash the phone back down so you don't have to listen to its empty ringing.

Don't cry. Stand up. Open the window. Feel the cold wind on your face; look to the horizon, at the city lights, and think of the people behind those lights, and wonder about them. Think of them and wish you could meet them. Yearn to meet them.

Yearn to meet him.

Slam the window shut. Fetch a jumper. Ignore the silent phone. Decide you don't need this. Decide to be empowered, uplifted, independent and strong. Decide that you don't need this, no, you don't need this, your mum must be right, and anyway you have your own life and your job and your friends and your hobbies, a whole, full, joyous life built up brick by painstaking brick and entirely and completely without him.

Let yourself wish, just a little, that he would have been there whilst you did all that building.

Try to remember if there's ice cream in the freezer. Remember that yes, there's definitely ice cream in the freezer. Check the flavour of the ice cream.

Make a face when you realise the box is empty with only a few curls left clinging to the plastic container. Remember that it was all eaten when you hosted your birthday dinner party a few weeks ago.

Crave ice cream, that sweet, cold treat on the tongue.

Call the Chinese place and ask them if they could add ice cream to your order. Swallow back tears when they say yes.

Pace the kitchen. Pick up a fruit from the fruit bowl then put it down again.

Consider calling your mum, then change your mind, knowing she did not approve and would not want to be involved.

Breathe in deeply.

Pick up the phone again. Dial the number again.

Wait.

Wait some more.

Breathe.

Hyperventilate.

Panic when the phone is picked up. Hang up. Bury your head in your hands.

Hear the doorbell ring. Answer the door.

Put the ice cream in the freezer to keep it cold and pick a film to watch before dishing out your Chinese.

Sit on the sofa and balance your plate on your knees. Put the plate down and unplug the phone then curl up again and pick up the takeaway. Eat. Try not to feel like a coward. Do not succeed. Try harder. Find good arguments to argue your case. Feel bad anyway.

Plug the phone back in.

Eat the Chinese, barely watching the film, eyes lost in a faraway daze. Think, as you sit there, that if you don't do this, you'll regret it forever, especially after all the time and effort put into convincing your mum to cough up the information. Put your plate down by your feet when it is empty and, dreamily, pick up the phone again.

Let your fingers dial the number.

Hold your breath.

Smile.

Say hello.

Listen to the voice at the end of the telephone. Hear the waver in the tone, the tremble behind the words and feel, suddenly, overwhelmed, taken by a great crashing wave that lifts you in its embrace and carries you forth, without even so much as a by-your-leave. Grip the telephone hard, so hard that your hand starts to tremble a little, and bite your lip, and take in a breath that is half-gasp and half-sob.

Hear the garbled explanation and don't even try to unpick it, just let the words flow over you as you listen to her voice. Listen to her voice and close your eyes and try to picture her, her face and her eyes, the shape of her face and the colour of her hair, whether she pouts like her mother did and whether she would have your jawline or even maybe your eyebrows.

Hope for her sake she doesn't have your eyebrows; they would look too harsh on a woman's face.

Hear the question but don't understand it, not yet, it is too big and too much and, dumbly, in a numb tone, ask her to repeat it. Listen to her as she has to pause, you know to swallow back tears, before she can ask you again to meet with her.

Say yes.

Say it again and feel the catch in the back of your throat.

Say yes.

Say yes, yes, you would love to, of course, of course you would love to, you want nothing else, nothing else could make you happier, and before you colours swim as your eyes fill with tears, relief, joy and pain all mingling together.

Hear her little bubble of wet laughter burst on the other end of the telephone and grin absurdly; grin at nothing as you clutch your telephone and stare at the smudged colours and listen to your daughter cry and laugh and laugh and cry on the other end of the telephone.

Inquire about the details, location, date and time. Feel relief that she is not far, only an hour and a half by train, and arrange to meet at the weekend in the town that is between the two of you, so that it is equal and fair, not one person having put forth more effort than the other to come to the meeting, so that it starts off on an equal footing. Feel pleased at that. Hear the relief in her voice, that she won't have to do all of the hard work and heavy lifting. Agree on a Saturday at two in the afternoon. Mention a tea shop you know, where you've been before and that you know quite well, where you're sure to enjoy the strong, black coffee, no stinting on the quality of the beans there, and the cakes are good too, not to forget the pub next door for a small jolt of liquid courage should you need it. Recommend the almond and blueberry frangipane tart, if she gets there before you. Hear the smile in her voice as she says that she loves blueberries, and frangipane, and tarts.

Say goodbye, no, not goodbye, but see you soon, see you very, very soon, and hang up the phone, feeling elated.

Think about your daughter. Think about your daughter and speculate, because she must be, oh, all of thirty-two now, and consider that it is just like her mother, just like her to keep that wonderful girl from you all this time.

Dwell bitterly on that for a moment, on that bitch, a cunt through and through, you had said it enough times and you were right enough, she was that and more besides, to keep a father from his daughter. Blame her for the psychological damage it must have caused. Feel sorry for the girl, to have to do without you all this time, and promise yourself you'll make it all better, now you're here and now you know and now you're going to meet her.

Go back into the kitchen and pick up your glass of beer. Drain it. Celebrate by pouring yourself another, because this is a special occasion and you want to celebrate it, and you will celebrate it, goddammit, black looks be damned.

Take a swig of beer, refusing to be cowed by her glare.

Ignore the acid remark about drinking on an empty stomach on a week day. Rise above the observation that tomorrow morning will be difficult. Be very patient and calm when she asks who was on the phone and why you look so pleased with yourself, like a cat that got the cream, like a fat, useless cat that's found someone else's mouse, so smug and licking your lips.

Tell her that it is none of her fucking business when she sticks her nose where it doesn't belong. Tell her to keep out of it when she insists, repeating who was on the phone, who was on the fucking phone, tell me, tell me, you bastard, who was on the phone.

Tell her when she rounds on you to just put dinner on the table, for God's sake. Tell her that she's making a fool of herself.

Wrinkle your nose when she opens the oven and a gust of black smoke wafts out. Slam down the empty glass of beer and cross your arms, because of course, of fucking course the bitch would find a way to ruin this special evening, this wonderful, precious event, of course she would sabotage it by burning dinner. Tell her so; reproach her with her passive aggressiveness and tell her you won't stand for it, not anymore, that you've had enough and that you don't know why you stay with such a useless, fat cow who can't even cook chicken without burning it.

Pour yourself another glass of beer, the can nice and cold from the fridge, chilling your fingers, and drink it, leaning against the counter as she cries. Study the bottom of your pint glass thoughtfully as she sobs, before becoming impatient with her artificial tears. Tell her to cut it out. Say it to her again, cut it the fuck out, and say you mean it. See her eyes widen and her gaze go to the pint glass and see her nod and gulp and wipe away the tears with her sleeve and set about putting the dinner on the table.

Nod. Grab a fork and spear a potato that you eat straight away, the fat running down the metal, burning your tongue and lips, saying good, that you can't be bothered to have another fight tonight, all right, that you've had a long, shit day and that you've just had some good news and that you want to celebrate in peace, goddammit, in goddamn peace without someone nagging and pecking at you and burning your dinner.

Sit down at the table and take another potato. Watch as she busies and bustles around the kitchen, all messy, curly hair and unmade face, the skin ageing, the sad little pouches of the cheeks pulling down and creases around her letterbox of a mouth, pulled up shut tight in a small, thin line. Look at the chicken and declare it to not be that bad, only burnt on one side, look, the other's barely charred. Carve the chicken and set the burnt bits aside generously, telling her they can go in the stock tomorrow. Smile indulgently when she nods and pats her face dry with her napkin. Look away politely when she pours herself glass of water and takes a gulp so that she can take her tablet more easily.

Spend the rest of the evening pleasantly enough, in the quiet and confident expectation that Saturday would go down as smoothly as the pint you're nursing.

Stare at the blueberry frangipane tart in front of you, all neat and pretty on its square, white porcelain plate. Finger the matching jug of cream that came with it, dainty with its pattern of bluebells and daisies and the little cap of yellow risen to the top of the liquid. Consider pouring it on top of the tart and watch it coat those purple little buds before bursting them with the attack of the fork but decide against it, pushing the plate away from you a little so that you won't be as tempted, because you don't want to start without him.

Wait.

Wait impatiently, your fingers playing with your necklace and tugging at your earrings. Pull out your compact to check your make up. Put it away again. Pull it out again and grope at the bottom of your handbag until you find your lipstick. Purse your lips and, carefully considering the cupid's bow reflected back at you; smear on the lippy, careful to get the edges. Press your lips together tightly, moving them back-and-forth a little so that the colour will be evenly distributed. Consider the effect in your reflection. Decide that it is perfect. Close the compact with a sharp snap.

Nab the waitress as she walks by and ask her if the clock on the wall is correct. Nod miserably when she tells you what you already know, that yes, it is correct, thank you very much, it is quarter-to-three. Ignore the look of pity she throws you when she sees the heavy make-up and the untouched tart and instead order another cup of tea, a special treat this time, a London Fog, please, and to hell with the calories, you need the comfort, the vanilla syrup like a warm hug around your chest.

Look around and realise everyone else in the coffee shop are in couples. Resent their happiness bitterly.

Have a wild bubble of joy rise up in your throat and threaten to strangle you when a man walks through the door. Settle down in your seat when his eyes sweep over you without recognition and go to another table, arms spread in a hug, his face lighting up. Pull out your phone and play on it until the burn of the humiliation has subsided a little.

Glance at the clock. Repress the jolt of anger when you see that five whole minutes have gone by. Look at your tart and consider digging into it since he doesn't have the decency to show up on time, the miserable bastard.

Pick up the cream jug. Put it down again. Cross your arms and sigh. Fidget.

Smile automatically when the waitress brings the cup of tea. Pick up your spoon and carefully harvest on the lip of the cutlery a nugget of vanilla scented foam. Savour it, eyes closed. Make it last.

Flinch when a gust of cold wind from the door envelops you. Open your eyes and see him, see him finally, standing there, muffled in a big, green coat, tartan scarf around his neck, his face flushed red from cold.

Recognise him instantly. Raise your hand to wave at him and call him over.

Hesitate, hand in mid-air. Watch him as he looks around, his eyes screwed up into shallow slits in his big red face, the nose almost a beak in profile, burst capillaries visible from even where you're sitting, and he's swaying, he's actually swaying as he's standing there, looking around the teashop to find you.

Smile awkwardly when he sees you and lumbers over. Panic when he reaches the table and extends both arms in the expectation of a hug. Offer your cheek instead and choke a little when he leans in close to kiss it and you can smell the booze on him.

Sit back down, that awful stiff smile on your face, and feel relieved when the waitress bustles over to take his order before either of you can say anything. Nod and keep smiling when he squints at your mug and plate and mumbles that he'll have the same thing as her, the exact same thing as his daughter.

Try to ignore that feeling inside. Comment on the cold weather outside and try not to launch yourself across the table and grab both shoulders to shake him, repressing the scream inside you, why are you so late why why why. Smile and ask about his journey. Try to keep smiling when he leans over and puts his hand on yours and the stink of him washes over you. Try not to look disgusted.

Fail. Watch the hurt in his eyes when he takes his hand away and mumbles something about meeting friends in a pub. Maintain the fixed rictus on your face when he peers at the clock and says something about losing track of time. Nod and pick up the cream jug, pouring it over the tart, regretting not doing it earlier, when it would have tasted sweeter whilst you were still in the happy bosom of expectation, and not buffeted by the cold winds of reality.

Pierce the fluffy golden top of it and bring the forkful to your mouth, nodding as he talks and talks and talks, going on about his life. Try not to dwell on the fact that he asks you nothing, not even your job or whether you're married or have children of your own, nothing about your life and your past and your present and your future.

Let the increasingly garbled words wash over you. Finish the tart and the London Fog and order another cup of tea, Earl Grey this time, thank you, ducking your head at the waitress' knowing look of sympathy.

Point at his tart, forgotten at his elbow, and hook it towards you with your index finger as he continues to unravel the chaotic fabric of his words. Pour the remainder of your cream onto it and start to eat, looking at him flatly and nodding occasionally.

Say nothing. Chew. Sit in silence.

Think.

Look at him. Notice the wear on the elbows of his jumper, the shine on the collar of his shirt, the dinginess of the scarf and the way the pattern clashes with his coat. Purse your lips disapprovingly at the shaving rash on his neck. Be faintly disgusted by the bags under his eyes, the jowls at his jaw, the broken web of red beneath the skin. Finish your food and wipe your hands on the napkins provided in a pernickety gesture, crumpling up the disposable item before dropping it onto your plate.

Look at the time and make an excuse, rising and gathering

up your coat, pulling out your purse to abandon several notes on the table, far more than is needed to pay the bill but whatever it takes to get rid of him and to get out of there relatively unscathed.

Ignore the bruised look on his face.

Walk, pulling on your coat, the sleeves settling around your arms, the handbag swinging into place like a sword, and push the door open and go through, letting it slam shut behind.

Walk. Walk and don't look back, pulling your chin up and high, breathing in that sharp, clean breath of air, moving forwards and onwards, always, leaving behind a weight and a waste with hardly a regret.

Walk and don't look back.

Salvage

MARTIN NATHAN

HORN OF PLENTY lurks by the path, its cracking black trumpet emerging from the leaf litter. Patches of clear ground struggle as the tangled grass takes hold again; you follow its line until all that is left is the rich smell of decay. In the dense part of the wood you hear rumbling; something is burrowing beneath the sinking ground and it will emerge if only you keep quiet long enough. But long enough is forever and your breath is catching up with you.

The hut in the clearing is painted blue, and underneath the blue it has flaked to watery yellow. And white, crumbling white. A bucket sits two steps high, overflowing with White Shield bottles, damp labels peeling; and Johnny Walker, all empties; and a coil of thick blue washing line that can't be cut, three pairs of grey school shorts have turned white from hanging there so long. Someone had said he'd seen the brown beer bottles full of blood, but they were empty now. Just a dribble of beer, mixed with rainwater. You can see a man with a black beard inside, eyebrows wild and tangled, eyes flashing every time his head turns. His face is picked out by the light of something hidden, the tremblings maybe of a candle, and he talks, shouts, at an imaginary person, or rehearses an argument for the evening, taking both sides. The argument goes on forever in silence.

Last time you'd taken fright, seeing those bottles, hearing his shouting.

The path from the road into the woodland was darker, and every time your family drove past on the B road your grandmother would look into the black wood and say, as if for the first time, 'That would be a good place to bury a body,' and you would all groan.

You heard the voices as your feet crunched leaves on the path, voices that whispered to you to turn back: 'Don't follow us.' But they were only voices in the ground beneath, and no-one listened to them. There were ructions in the soil, as if a life had been about to break through, but changed its mind.

On the ridge you could see the motorway where a lorry had pushed half into the grass embankment. The back was open and a gang of kids emerged with white boxes, triumphantly flinging candles and soap into the air, onto the tarmac. Or down the grass embankment as far as they could. A siren sounded, and in the approach of the flashing blue light the kids disappeared. As if they were never there. The police car paused beside the lorry before shooting off, light flashing but silent.

The back of that lorry was a dark, black box that contained anything you could imagine; if you slid down the slope and made sure you hid. Kept an eye open for police cars. Sometimes unmarked. They put their hands in but the good stuff was always just out of reach. When they were done, there were blackberries and small sweet apples on the tree by the path.

You watched them. In the distance.

And they said that he'd give you beer if you were there in the afternoon. He would stand at the gate holding two bottles, but only one opened, saying nothing, waiting. You just had to take him a gift, something he needed, living in a hut in the woods. Soap and candles. But if he needed them so much where did the beer come from? Where did he get all that stuff in the hut?

You never knew anyone who'd been there before for definite except the McGuire twins and they were tough and fought like tigers until Sam threw his brother through the first-floor window and cut a vein in his own arm doing it. You stood with him in collective horror, as the blood ran down his arm onto damp earth, forming a darker puddle on the water collected there. Light glinting off hard angled glass and soft water. Sam was shouting through the window, silver daggers pointing up to his chest. The McGuire rage they called it. Red hair. Red rage. Angry at something and nothing. Shouting, what was he shouting? They'd been to the hut. You'd smelt the beer on those boys' breath; they weren't lying. So it couldn't be true, everything people said.

You'd heard about the boys chased by the police, another police car cutting them off between the abattoir and the fields of the open prison where the grass cut your legs. They ran fast through the fields but the police were relentless. Gasping but relentless.

You'd watched as they were marched, still clutching the candles and soap on the walk of shame with the whole school at lunch, to the Headmaster who was entertaining a distinguished guest, a councillor and business man, probably a Freemason with secret punishments for thieving. You couldn't help feeling a bit jealous, a bit like you wished you were with them, sharing their fear, their notoriety, holding the stolen goods. They'd said they'd take you with them but they didn't. Left you waiting. Now their lies were relentless, breathless with fear, but cut off mid-word, in front of the parade of green and white, boxes of candles and fairy liquid.

There is a whisper that you can hear from someone you used to know well, whose face is hidden in the trees, in the forms in the bark, in the shapes the leaves make. On the tree a line of Jew's Ear's brown rubber and you can tell there's stinkhorn, somewhere poking through the ground. You have forgotten their name but you want to see their face once more. To hear their voice. In the silence.

Along that path in the woodland you can hear the jackdaw crying, coarse and thuggish, and you want to go to that door, knock on that wooden paneling with the crumbling paint, to stop the muted shouting even though you have no gift, no roadside treasure to trade for a beer. You want to leave it all behind, to drink beer, not just sips, to drink it properly, gulp it down. To taste whisky. Feel it burn your throat. The taste of oblivion. The clearing.

The bare earth gives a little. The leaves crunch down, leaving the marks of your trail, dark in the woods, but still clearly visible in torch light when they come looking.

The Consultant

JIM LEWIS

YOU ARE WATCHING your child die. There is nothing you can do. You wait and watch as the nurse comes in and checks the drip, fills in the chart and asks you if you want a cup of tea. She comes close, places her hand gently on Eileen's forehead. She turns to go, but halts in the doorway. You stop your rocking back and forth.

"Mr Khan will be along afterwards... this afternoon... to talk to you, Mr Kelly and your wife."

You nod a thank you to her.

"Martha... Mrs Kelly, will be here after her work." You say. "As soon as she's finished in the school kitchen."

Mrs Flaherty will pick up the other wain after school. You are not looking forward to what the consultant has to say. You put your head in your hands. Shame again coming upon you, for how you manhandled Fr. O'Dowd. But with his smug ways he had it coming.

"Mr Kelly, it may be that God has chosen your Eileen to be with him and our Blessed Mother and be spared the sully of this vale of tears," the priest had said.

Your hands had him by the throat before your head knew it. The Guard that had come along from the Kesh, pulled you off him. Now the screw sits, there in the corner, pretending to read the *Belfast Telegraph*. His big body bulges over the chair. He told you there is an armed RUC man outside the door. The screw's eyes flicker on you. Your own are moist. The cuffs make it hard to rub away and hide the rising tears.

"Chosen by God?"

How could a loving God choose a nine-year-old girl? You reach for Eileen's hand. Her wrists are stalks now. Once at Portrush, in Water World, those small hands had clung round your neck as you'd set off down the slide. The lifeguard had told you off and once out of sight of him you had both laughed at the small act of shared wickedness.

After your arrest, you thought at first that her becoming thinner was her keening for you. The weekly visits seemed to be taking their toll on her and Martha. Getting so early to the Sinn Fein office on the Falls for the Minibus, and then the long journey to see you, seemed to be draining the life out of her, the fire in her red hair fading. But Seamus didn't seem to notice anything, not the searches nor the clashing of doors, nor the turning of keys. He'd sit on the floor playing with a racing car or colouring in his book. Eileen seemed sad, pale and thinner on each visit. Then, that time Martha came without the children, you knew it was bad. She burst into tears as she entered the visitor space and saw you. They wouldn't let you touch her or comfort her.

So now you wait for Mr Khan, the consultant. It is strange how the consultant is always a Mister. They must have climbed to the top of the heap and dropped the need for the honour of being called Doctor. You wonder if the queen was ever called plain Mrs Windsor. Now that is an odd thought to you, to learn everything and know so much you become a plain Mister again.

Eileen stirs for a moment and whimpers. You long to cradle her in your arms, the way you did that time when she fell asleep in the back of the car and they made you get out at the checkpoint at Aughnacloy. You would not have her wakened. You stood and watched and she slept across your shoulder as they took the car apart. Then, when they finished, with everything you owned out on the ground, they'd leave you to put it back. You'd settle her down on the back seat and the soldiers would be looking, watching and laughing between themselves. You couldn't make out a face. They were shadows with guns and you were a blinded rabbit in the glare of their floodlights.

They knew who you were and what you believed. So, you took their payback, but you would protect Eileen.

It was Mr Khan who had told Martha it was Leukaemia, had told her that recovery rates were better than they were twenty years before. But you knew what Cancer was. As a child, it was like a dirty word, an evil that came upon you if it ever entered your mouth. Cancer, Brit, grass, Crown forces, they all brought evil with them, but Leukaemia, the word has a soft lull to it, like it was something that sends you off into dreamy sleep, so that you never come back.

Martha had brought a leaflet that told about blood cells and marrow and all the great work going on at the Royal Victoria and elsewhere and the world-famous doctors, right here in the North, that were breaking new boundaries, that in a year or two would result in a cure.

You think back to the night they lifted you. You knew you had fouled up. They took swabs so they knew you'd been handling. You kept quiet; you felt shame that you'd fouled up and that closed your mouth tighter. If it had been a General, a Lord or an Earl you'd have proudly spilled the beans, taken the whole wrap and protected the others. So, in the end, all they could put you away for, was handling.

You'd walked in that part of North Belfast a dozen times that week. You'd seen the dark green BMW outside the gardened Square near Queens. You walked past where it would be parked, knew when it would be there and for how long. You learned the escape routes. It is easy to be invisible; you become part of the scene. You had a wad of leaflets to push through every letter box, for double glazing, a new bar and whatever else they got for you. The streets there were well used to you coming and going.

From what you learned, it was you that chose the time, when few students would be about. There were no cameras in that part of the street and you'd practised the tying of laces by the target. But the street light was blinking and fading that night and the street was dark, as you bent down to tie your shoe, and stick the device under the car, and then to pull the cord gingerly, to arm it. In the dark it was an easy mistake.

Black can look dark green. You fouled up. So, when the blast came you were far enough away to be seen running back. Never run away, that's what the guilty do. The scared freeze and cower. The good, the helpers, the compassionate run back, run towards.

They cordoned off the scene. They expected another bomb to catch the arriving Brits. This time there would be no second one. They told you to disperse and you caught the bus from the Botanic Gardens and then a black cab up the Falls to Anderson Town, and safety. But somewhere a camera caught you. They had suspicions. The hooding and beating didn't help them. You were silent because you were shamed. They kept you awake and in the morning, they flung the newspaper in front of you.

It was the one from the dark corner that spoke. The one not in uniform. Him with the English voice.

"See what you have done? Killed a good man."

The one who'd beaten you in the cell, now held your head between his hands from behind. He was strong and he held you in his vice.

"There's no good Englishman!" you shouted.

He smashed your face onto the table and he pulled your head back by the hair. Blood from your nose dripped on the smiling picture of a middle-aged man and below it a picture of three girls and a woman and the same smiling man.

The English voice called, "Enough!"

You read:

Consultant Dr Arthur Forbes was killed yesterday by what is believed to be an IRA bomb. Dr Forbes was a world-renowned cancer expert with a special interest in childhood Leukaemia. His loss will be a great blow to the international community engaged in this area of research.

You remember you said. "I'm sorry for him."

"Sorry?" said the voice.

"Sorry, but there's a war on."

"You people." The voice said, "You people..."

Martha comes in. There is a female screw with her. She searches Martha and does not allow you to embrace. You notice that Eileen is struggling for breath.

The nurse opens the door. An Indian looking man, in a suit, enters. You catch a glimpse of a priest behind him. A different priest. He is in the grey robe of a Franciscan.

"I asked him to come." Martha says. "The friar..."

He follows her and stands by the window. He nods to each in the room.

The Consultant bows his head before he looks up. He breathes in and you struggle to cover your ears. The cuffs only shut him half out. He has nothing to say that you want to hear...

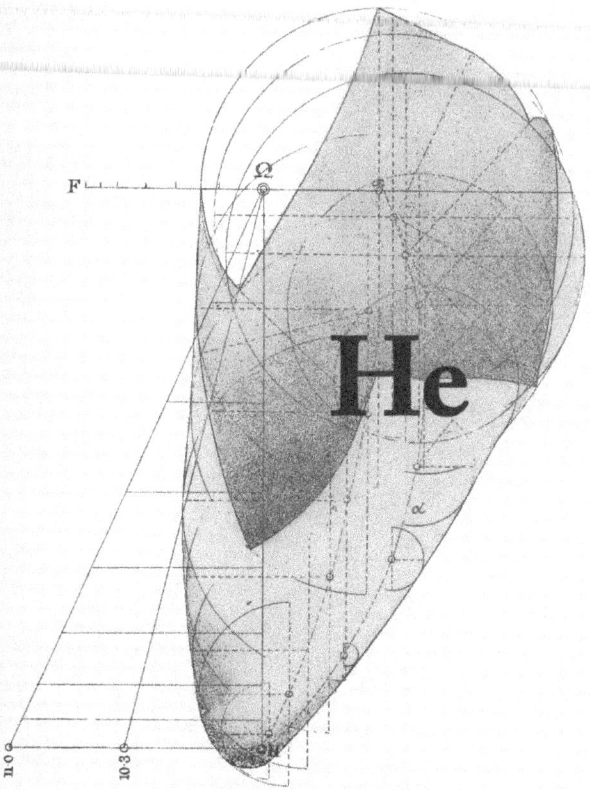
He
F
Ω
α
11·0
10·3

Martin's Sperm

MARK KENNY

HE SPRAWLED ACROSS the sofa in dirty white sports socks, boxers and an old t-shirt with holes in it. He scratched at his crotch, then brought his finger up and rubbed the stubble on his top lip. There was no-one else in the flat. He sniffed his fingers properly.

Cheese. Most probably from the huge bag of Doritos on his chest, which he intended to fold into a tight, precise triangle when it was empty and leave on the floor. He sighed, reaching down for his beer.

TV was alright at three in the morning. *Family Guy* and *American Dad* episodes back to back. All repeats. He'd seen them a hundred times before but the routine was comforting. Framed his day. Something mindless to burn through the hours before he felt tired enough to sleep.

He sipped the beer, angling his head so he wouldn't have to sit up, and became aware of the ache in his neck. The can fell over as he put it down, beer glugging out onto the carpet. He swore, fumbling to get it upright again, and managed to knock it under the sofa. While he was retrieving it he found a sheet of paper, now sodden. He remembered he'd put it there three weeks ago to keep safe.

Dear Mr Hunt, Following our consultation on the fifth... blah blah blah... *we regret to confirm...* blah blah blah... *standard compensation under the terms of the waiver...*

He sighed again. They'd explained the risks when he signed up. He'd dismissed the possibility of anything happening, eager to get the payout. It would clear all his debts with a bit left-over. They hadn't told him how many other men had taken part in the trial and he wondered if anyone else had 'suffered adverse reactions'. He told himself he didn't want kids anyway. He stopped himself screwing up the letter into a soggy ball. He might need it for the claim.

The last episode ended. He watched the credits to the end, not ready for the silence. There was a documentary on next about soldiers in Afghanistan. Gritty reality presented by some former soap actor. Blokes being blokey in sand-coloured uniforms. Penis-themed nicknames. Banter. Then shouts of "Contact!" and shaky footage of the camera operator's feet running for cover.

He stabbed at the TV with the remote and looked round at the room.

"Time for bed," he announced, trying to sound cheerful.

He took a leak, didn't bother brushing his teeth. There was nothing pressing to do the next day.

He woke up suddenly, convinced he wasn't alone in the room. There was something cold and wet on his cheek. Probably spit. He wiped it away and lay still, listening.

Nothing. He laughed to himself and rolled over.

Then, as he was drifting off, he heard a thump. All the hairs on his arms and the back of his neck stood on end. Then the sound of something sliding over carpet. He thought he saw the blankets twitch. He wasn't sure what to do but a rising panic and the pressure in his bladder convinced him to move. He inched across the mattress. The bed creaked.

Whatever was under there started crashing about like an animal caught in a trap. He jumped out of bed, fumbled with the door, and ran into the bathroom. He locked it, pausing for a moment, then pissed noisily into the toilet. He sat down and looked around for something to use as a weapon.

A few minutes later he was listening outside his bedroom door, clutching a bottle of spray cleaner dusty from lack of use.

He burst into his room brandishing the bottle, pointing it left and right like a cop in a crime drama.

The room was empty.

This is ridiculous, he thought. It's just a mouse or something. He flipped the duvet up with his foot and stepped back. Nothing. He got down on all fours and put his head under the bed. On the other side, a long white tail was slithering away from him. He went cold and couldn't move. The tail curled upwards and over the top of the bed. After it disappeared he became aware of something right next to his face. He looked at it out of the corner of his eye.

At first he thought it was a snake, but the head was too big, almost the same size as a rugby ball. It was milky white and shiny like it was made out of glass. There were no facial features of any kind.

The thing twitched. He tried to stand up but fell over backwards, dropping the spray cleaner. He scrambled to get away and banged his head on the wardrobe. The thing followed him as he went, gently snaking through the air. He screwed up his eyes waiting for an attack but it never came. When he opened them the opaque white had cleared. The inside of its head was bustling like a rock pool.

There was a central mass, larger and darker than anything else, wrapped in folds of gently billowing material. Tiny bubbles were coming and going from it, moving along a delicate network of chains connecting all the different parts. There were structures that looked like sheets of lace, others that looked like rough pieces of gravel, and others smooth like blobs of oil.

The thing came forward very slowly and grazed his cheek, then backed off to a corner of the ceiling and engaged in something that looked like preening. He sat up and wiped the dampness from his face. He stared at the thing on the ceiling, fascination displacing fear. He wondered if it was some kind of alien. It must be. There was no animal on earth it resembled. It was like a balloon on a long string. A giant white tadpole, or a—

"No, it couldn't be."

The creature stopped preening and looked over at him.

"But how… "

He stood there staring. It looked back for a while, then settled, slowly turning milky again, tucking its head into the loops of its tail. He had absolutely no idea what to do, but suddenly he was exhausted. He'd think about it in the morning, and tonight he'd sleep on the couch. He pulled the duvet off the bed and grabbed a couple of pillows. On his way out he picked up the spray bottle. The chemicals might be harmful. As he left he very gently closed the door so as not to wake it.

Over the next couple of weeks he got used to having it around. Naturally, he couldn't have anyone over. But he never had anyone over anyway, so that wasn't a problem. He began to look forward to coming in after a long night's work. His new friend was becoming a part of his life.

"We need to give you a name," he said one evening. "Are you male or fe— well, I suppose you're male. I wonder if you already have one, back wherever it is that you're from. Hey, buddy?"

They were in the lounge. They often watched TV together these days. It looked at him and cocked its head.

"How about we just settle on Buddy?"

The Fear Of Your Own Reflection

MICHAEL HARGREAVES

HE PASSED UNNOTICED through the bodies on the high street, like a ghost. Tate was beside himself, walking. There was a familiar weight to the air. It was as if the world had exhausted itself and was leaning on him in its entirety. I had the advantage of being able to see the past and present, as one. From the right, I could see his past. He was pulled forward by his chest and each step claimed whatever ground it touched. But from the left, I saw him now, burying his gaze in the pavement. His shoulders were slightly hunched forward and his arms folded around a large brown envelope. It reminded me of all the patients I'd visited over the years. After just a few months of wearing a straitjacket, the muscles adjust to the pose and the only comfort they can find is in that position. Tate, like many before him, was 'fixed'.

I joined him again as he stepped into Ben's office. Ben managed only two or three acts, including Tate. His office was always filthy. Every time Tate had visited, the bin had not been emptied and the small flip-book calendar on his desk was a few days behind. Although Tate hadn't actually been to the office in the last six months, the routine never changed. Ben always pretended to be on the phone as his acts walked in. He'd then wave Tate in to sit down while he wrapped up the conversation, spending at least two minutes doing so.

"Sorry about that. Producers – you know?" he joked. "How was-" Ben glanced to his computer screen before continuing, "-that play, the audition?"

"It was fine. I only came by to drop off these headshots." Tate placed the envelope on Ben's cluttered desk. I knew what Ben was thinking. *Why have you made more headshots? You look the same as ever. I'm only going to use the ones you sent me last time.*

"Great!" He smiled. "Let's have a look."

Tate's eyes found themselves focusing in on Ben's fingertips as they moved slower and slower the more he noticed them. When they finally reached the envelope a strange fear came over him. He almost reached out to take the envelope back, but didn't. The crunch of the paper as Ben picked up the envelope, slit straight through his spine. When the envelope was ripped open Tate's body began to ache. He fought against himself by gripping the sides of the chair and tightening his muscles, refusing the urge to fold into himself like a car being crushed into a square. Ben dragged the headshots out of the envelope and looked at them in shock.

After a few seconds flicking between the pictures, he whispered, "I'll get these out."

The next time I saw Tate was in his home. The shop windows on the high street, the photo frame on Ben's wall – I'll give him this, he was doing well to avoid me. His house was in steady decline; stamped-out cigarette ashes were smudged like rain clouds into his carpet and a collection of circular coffee stains overlapped each other across the arms of his sofa. His knees creaked as he lowered himself into the cushions. He took out a pack of cigarettes. Only recently had the comfort of smoke set in, feeling like fresh air in and out of his lungs. I felt my chest being touched. *At the same time, Ben's fingertips brushed across the laminate of the headshots, pushing them to one side.* Tate's face became another piece of clutter on his desk, buried beneath another.

Tate watched the phone ring for a few seconds; it was Grace. He considered not answering. She'd already called him a few times today. He decided that he owed her at least one minute of conversation. As Tate spoke to her he began to think about the last time they'd had sex. She had come over after the closing night of the play they co-starred in.

"Amazing – they said! Did you read it?" her voice squeaked through the phone.

"I heard it was good. You got a mention didn't you?"

"Yeah, they said my performance was *elatedly reserved!"*

Tate took the phone away from his mouth and sighed out smoke. He wasn't even sure how that was possible. He joked to himself about whether or not you could call Grace's acting a performance at all. I would have told him that his own was not much better, that night.

"Yeah, I remember reading that," he lied, "What are you doing now then?" he stubbed the cigarette out.

"What, right this second or generally?" she giggled.

Tate rolled his eyes and continued,

"Both, I suppose." He picked at the coffee stains as if they were scabs.

"Well, I've got an audition next week for a part in this new drama – honestly, you need to get yourself over to television. You're good looking enough for it – and right this second, I'm just on my own in my house." Her tone dropped off towards the end of the sentence as if she was trying to dim the lights on the conversation.

"Sounds lonely," he said, grinning slightly.

"It is…" She whispered. "You could come and keep me company if you wanted? We could celebrate the review…"

He'd never been to Grace's house before. It was much better kept than his and had actually been decorated by Grace herself. Tate had simply moved into a furnished house and never bothered to make it a home. It didn't take her long to make the first move. She leaned over and started to kiss Tate. He felt unusually nervous. He was not the same human he used to be – as much as he could pretend he was, depending on the company at hand. Grace placed her hand on his wrist and guided it up to her hips, like a puppeteer. I began to wonder if it mattered that Tate was Tate at all; maybe he was just on-call that day.

I found them again when they entered her room. There was nowhere for me to see them on their way upstairs. Tate's eyes were closed. He was bending down slightly, making himself short enough to kiss Grace. He started unbuttoning his shirt. His muscles were still well defined even though he'd dropped his very precise and intense fitness regime. When his eyes opened, all his confidence vanished. He looked at the side of her bed. The wall was completely covered in mirrors. I stared at him and he was forced to stare back for the first time in six months. I could see myself through his eyes. The skin beneath my chin swung like an empty noose, my arms were strangled in varicose veins and there was a growing death around my eyes. He panicked and pulled at his neck. Frantic and beside himself again, he pulled and pulled but his skin felt fine. As she took off his shirt and started kissing his chest, he could only stare over her head at me. Her teeth bit into me and the loose flesh draped over her face like mouldy leather. Tate pushed away from Grace – afraid she could see.

"What's wrong?" she asked.

He stood before her, but still he couldn't take his eyes off me. Grace turned her head to the mirror and smiled.

"Alright, Narcissus – come here."

She sat down on the bed facing him, opened her legs and pulled him towards her. He tried to ignore me, but there was no-where to hide. He watched as a patch of my wrinkled flesh faded away, leaving only the reflection of the wall behind him. *Ben threw one of the headshots in the bin.* Tate felt a chill crawl through his stomach where I had vanished. Grace stared up at him.

"Tate, what's the problem?" She looked at him with her eye brows pulled together in disgust.

He shook his head. He felt another chill down the left side of his face. He watched as mine dissolved. *The second photo fell.* Grace stood up. Tate didn't hear what she said. *The third and fourth scraped against each other.* He lost all feeling in his body that wasn't physical. He watched helplessly. Grace said something again. *Ben's fingertips grasped the last photo.* Tate suddenly returned to the room.

"If we're not going to do this could you just say so? I'm barely in the mood now." Grace hissed.

Tate couldn't even look at her. *Ben dropped the last headshot.* The last of me disappeared. Tate's stomach fell like an anchor through water; his heart, the bow, was pulled under too.

A Real Purple Patch

RUSSELL READER

HE'D BEEN AWAKE since half-past five, holding it in, jigging, twitching, trying desperately not to wake his brother and sister who he shared the mattress with, or – worse – his dad, who was snoring in the bed in front of the window, his bulky body hardly a foot away, rising and falling to a soundtrack of whistles and heavy sighs.

Sam refused to use the bedpan, though nobody else seemed to mind it – their urine fermenting like punch at a party until his mam swilled it all down the drain the next morning with a bit of carbolic.

A thunderstorm of hot piss hit the freezing pan of the shared outside toilet, washing off a stranger's skids and leaving the seat peppered with yellow pearls. That'll teach them, Sam thought, as he tore the last square of newspaper off the string and scrunched it up into a ball. Dirty bastards.

He was out of the house before seven; they all were. Mary and George – younger than him, only two and four – went to Nana's next door. Sam walked with his mam and dad to the mill at the bottom of the street; his dad going down to the warehouse, him and his mam climbing up the stone stairs to the spinners where they'd stay until six.

His dad spent Saturdays in the con club. Sam spent them entertaining Mary and George, wandering around town with them until the bakery put the *Half Price Bread* sign in the window just before closing. Quick, grab it. This particular Saturday – this lifeless, shivering Saturday – seemed to go on and on and on. As he loitered on the high street, his siblings playing hopscotch as he patrolled the precinct; both eyes locked on the bakery, he felt something under his shoe. Hard, solid. He instinctively dropped, pretending to tie his laces. It glimmered in the winter sun as he moved his foot slightly, making him squint.

He'd never seen a pound coin before, never felt one in his palm. His whole body shook as he twirled it around in his pocket, hoping that nobody had noticed him pick it up, his hands sweaty, his heart racing. He strode straight into the bakery and bought the bread at full price – two loaves this week – then went to the grocers next door. *Half a pound of cheese please, and six slices of that ham.* A block of Dairy Milk for his mam, the newspaper for his dad, a bottle of pop for Mary and George – and a roll of Andrex for himself.

His mam's eyes lit up when he told her what had happened. She grabbed plates from the cupboard and starting laying the table, excitedly humming show tunes, the spring back in her step. Mary and George ran around her legs, giddy at the thought of a mouthful of pop. Then his dad walked in.

The pop bottle smashed against the grate, specks of sarsaparilla flying into the flames and making the fire spit and crackle. He threw the brown paper bag against the wall, a heavy thud of ham and bread and chocolate and newsprint and toilet roll bouncing off it in different directions, then he turned and glared at Sam, his round face pumping with crimson veins, like a balloon that was about to pop. *You should have given it to me,* he roared.

Sam gingerly tore five sheets off the roll before he went outside the next morning, folding them up neatly. He sat on the broken seat, watchful of the daddy longlegs on the ceiling and the cobwebs in the corner, and traced his fingers over the blue and mauve splodges on his thighs. When he'd finished he took the sheets out from his pocket, unfolding them onto his lap with delicate fingers, like a historian might unfurl a rare tapestry, and wiped them softly against his skin. He'd never felt anything like it. *This is the life,* he whispered, under his breath.

This is the life.

Lucky Dress

JO HILEY

HE FOLLOWS HER into the petrol station and parks up nearby. He walks towards the kiosk and as he passes she swears as she fumbles with the petrol cap. He thinks she's perfect, fat and old, her thin dress pulled tight over her body, the straps of her bra cutting into her flesh. He stands in the queue and watches her through the window as she replaces the hose and tightens the cap. When she bends down to reach for her bag on the passenger seat her dress rides up exposing bare, dimpled flesh. She walks towards the kiosk. It's late; the only other customers are men, most of them taxi drivers. A few look her up and down; one of them smiles at her. She lowers her head and walks by.

He picks up some chewing gum and hands the money to the man behind the counter. When he turns back around she is coming through the door. He walks towards her and drops his keys at her feet. He bends to get them, looks up, smiles and says sorry for getting in her way. She blushes, says its OK. He starts to walk out then turns back and catches her watching him. She turns away quickly and pays for her petrol.

Back outside he reaches into his pocket then drops down by her car pretending to tie his shoelace. He plunges a knife into the wall of her tyre and hears a slight hiss as the air begins to slowly leak out. He gets back into his car and waits for her to climb into hers. She looks over to him and smiles. He smiles back waiting for her to pull away and follows. She doesn't drive far before she notices her tyre is flat. She pulls over, puts her hazard lights on and gets out of the car. She looks at the damage. He pulls alongside her, rolls down the window, says can he help. Her face lights up; she's thrilled its him, a friendly face. He parks up in front of her car, climbs out and walks towards her. He says she's lucky, he's a mechanic; it's no bother at all to help her out. He's changed hundreds of tyres in his time. If he had a pound for every one he'd be a rich man.

She opens the boot and shows him the spare. Do me a favour he says, go and get the torch out of the glove box. She hurries off. He takes the knife from his pocket and stabs the spare several times; the air hisses out. She hands him the torch. Bad news, he says; looks like the spare's flat, nothing he can do tonight. He says he can tow it for her first thing in the morning. I can give you a lift home, he says; can't have a lovely lady like her stranded in the middle of nowhere, wouldn't want her husband worrying. Yes please, she says, if its no trouble. No trouble at all, he says. He can see she can't believe it's happening to her. She's not married, she says, just her and the cat at home. That's a lovely dress, he says. She blushes. She'll have to call it her lucky dress from now on.

She locks her car and climbs into his passenger seat. When she turns to pull over the seatbelt her dress rides up her bare thighs. She doesn't pull it back down. Where to, he says. Just carry on to the next village and she'll tell him where to turn, she says.

Stirring Of The Wind

JOHN BERESFORD

HE LEANED ON his rake and surveyed the results of his efforts. Nine neat piles, the dark green grass between them virtually free of leaves save for where one or two had escaped the pull of the tines and fallen from the path of the rake. He breathed deep of the autumn scents and smiled. The year was not yet old enough to have a winter chill, but had left summer far behind. Mornings like today – mist-shrouded and mysterious, damp and cool – were his favourites. One could do a day's work without breaking sweat and have time left in the still lengthy evenings to enjoy the view, or sit on the deck and savour a glass of wine.

A gust of wind teased his hair as he stood looking over the valley. A few leaves from the tallest piles shook themselves loose and fluttered away onto the grass. He pulled a plastic garden sack from his pocket and began stuffing it with leaves, anxious to complete the clearing up before the wind undid his day's work. As he grabbed handful after handful of the leathery brown leaves their sweet musky odour filled his nostrils, shaking loose memories of school mornings when he and Kate would kick their way to class, scattering the yellow, red and brown threads of the road rug with their polished patent leather, creating new patterns and shapes as the leaves flew and fell, flew and fell. Laughing at the gentle soughing and the smells and the joyous feeling of togetherness, the excitement of a new year ahead. New knowledge and new possibilities, coupled with pangs of old yearning. Wondering whether this would be the year she would start to look at him as more than the boy next door. Kate of the autumn-red hair and brown, gold-flecked eyes that shone and flashed as she laughed at his silly jokes. He played the clown for her to hide his longing. Cracked a joke to mask his embarrassment at the strength of feeling inside him. Stole a sidelong glance at the wonderful curves of her growing body. And fought down the need to declare himself in love with her, for fear of frightening her away.

The wind spoke again, and the trees answered. Sighing and rustling. He dashed away a tear with his gloved hand, the suede rough against his cheek. He knotted his bag, stood, and surveyed the garden once again. The few tentative gusts had blurred the edges of his piles, flattening and spreading them out. Sending handfuls of carefully collected leaves back out across the grass. Another few years and it would be too much for him to manage on his own, especially at this time of year. Too many trees, too much grass. And way too many memories. He always knew the leaves would unlock his past. Like evil spirits flying from Pandora's box, those bitter-sweet rememberings were always set free at this time of year. The season in which he'd had Kate, and the same season he'd lost her. The world had lost her. Like walking into a winter that never ended, and all that was left was cold and dark, crisp and bleak and featureless like a land buried beneath a lifetime of snow. Where Spring could never come

Michael, 38

FAYE CHAMBERS

He kicked him in the face, then placed a handkerchief over his mouth, making the captive pass out long enough to get him ready. Michael did the nails first, clipping the edges and filing the centre into sharp points. His clothes were removed next. There were patches where Michael had to tease the material away from where it had stuck to the flesh, still bleeding from the struggle. Finally he placed the black collar around the neck, neatly fastening the buckle and unfurling the leash. Michael stood back and looked on, satisfied.

He secured the leash to the hook on the wall and bound the wrists and ankles. After all, he didn't want his pet to run away.

"Are you gay or summat?" the cretin said, groggily, as he awoke.

His collar was tightened for that. Never in his life had Michael been so insulted. He kicked the beast once again, and spat into his bloody face. He left, locking the manbeast in the loft.

No. He was not gay. He went to the music room and burned all of his Elton John records, just in case.

Alice, 37, never expected anyone to respond to her ad. In fact part of her had hoped they wouldn't. But when Michael, 38, wrote to say how amazing it was to find a partner who shared his passion for photography, animals and crocheting, she couldn't believe her luck.

She finished plaiting her hair and tied it with a baby blue

ribbon to match her cardigan. She remembered how Michael had said he liked her blue cardigan on their first date. That was almost three months ago now.

"This could really be it," she said to her cat, nuzzling its ears with her delicate ivory hands. "Goodbye Mr Snufflekins," she called, and left, locking the door behind her.

As she approached she felt nervous – she had never been to Michael's house before. But he welcomed her with his winning smile and she felt at once like she was home. They sat and talked, fondly, as they always did. On Alice's request they had been taking the relationship slowly. She grew embarrassed as Michael edged closer to her, and in a panic, excused herself to the bathroom.

She took some time to calm herself down. Finally, she plucked up the courage to go back downstairs and join Michael. She was ready to take the next step. She dragged her timid feet out from the shelter of the bathroom and headed for the stairs.

But she stopped.

Alice stood, frozen. She could hear words creeping their way down from the loft above and into her ears, her mind.

"Help me," they said.

"Run," she thought, but her legs didn't listen.

There was a thud, and the voice slithered closer, a snake in the grass. Then silence.

It appeared suddenly, startling Alice. It was a face which resembled the face of a man, but could not have been. The thinning dark hair was matted and falling out in patches, the way it does on a stray cat. All light had been extinguished from its manic, grey eyes. Snarling jaws revealed the owner of the voice. A voice that wasn't really a voice at all, just ragged air rattling through the hollow shell of where a man's face should have been.

Alice felt hot and cold all at once. She looked upon the creature, fearing, pitying, and she thought the sight of it may drive her mad. The ringing of the voice inside her head deafened her to the footsteps coming from below. Shiny black shoes announcing their fanfare on a polished oak floor. Ascending the stairs to Alice purposefully, each 'clip clop' kept the tempo with clinical precision.

Michael felt a little dejected. He had liked Alice; she had nice feet. He had much grander plans for her than this. But it did not matter. The man beast had been seen. It must be dealt with.

The creature began wailing, putrid, animal sounds unlike anything she had ever heard before. It cowered against the magnolia wall, staining it with sweat, and cradled skeletal arms around its wilting body. The fear and hatred emanating from its gaze was directed somewhere over Alice's right shoulder. She felt a cold hand upon her back. Michael's hand. Spit started pooling in her mouth, and she barely resisted the urge to vomit.

"Ah, Alice..." he said, playfully. Sickeningly. "I see you've met my pet."

Michael reached between the sheltering arms of the creature and pulled on a black leather cord, which curved its way across the torso and up around its neck. Alice looked upon the collar and understood.

***

For three days, Alice had been trussed up like a turkey on Michael's bed. He had taken away her clothes, and bound her with thick red ropes that ate into her soft pale skin. Four times a day he came to photograph Alice, experimenting with different lighting. He decided dawn was his favourite. He liked to watch the shadows dancing on the wall as her body squirmed in the half light. On the dawn of the third day, he had knelt at the foot of the bed and began to lick Alice's feet, exploring the gaps between her toes with his tongue. But he did not touch her anywhere else. After all, he was not a monster.

The fourth day was a Tuesday. Alice's screams had torn up her throat like an old newspaper, and were now only occasional whimpers. The manbeast had not been fed for six days. It was time.

When he cut the ropes from around her limbs, Alice dared to hope that she would be freed, but that hope was misplaced. She felt the familiar tang of bile rising in her throat as Michael led her to the foot of the loft stairs where the manbeast dwelled.

As they approached the door she could hear him scratching, clawing at the wood between them. Michael opened the padlock and pushed a reluctant, shivering Alice inside.

She locked eyes with the manbeast, his grey stare more disturbing than the last time their gaze had met. The creature still seemed hollow, devoid of humanity, but starvation and madness had taken hold. Eyes that were once vulnerable now peered at her with unmistakable bloodlust. The beast was hungry.

"Hush now my precious one," he cooed. So calmly. "Dinner time."

And then it began.

Michael made a circular incision around her left breast, and peeled the skin back from the flesh as though it were an orange. He put it to his lips and toyed with it, as though it were the breast of a lover. Or at the very least, still attached to a human. The manbeast tried to break free from his chains and claim his meal, panting with anticipation.

"Beg," Michael demanded of the snarling beast at his heel. It obliged.

He inhaled deeply, then tossed it to the beast, who tore at it wildly with his jaws, howling like a jackal. As Michael put the knife to the right breast, Alice's body was overwhelmed by convulsions of pain and terror. She kicked out, at nothing in particular, and Michael slammed his body into her fragile leg, shattering the bone.

As the snarls grew louder, she heard a loosening of chains, the panic rising in her like the heat of an Indian summer. All at once the claws and limbs and teeth and sweat of the beast were upon her. Their eyes met one final time as the creature lunged for Alice's jugular in a frenzy, and she passed out.

***

Four months later, Michael was sat in his squashy armchair enjoying a nice cup of tea. He glanced at the framed picture of Alice on the mantelpiece – day two, twilight – sighed contentedly, and took a bite of his toast.

There was a flapping in the letter box, followed by some

grunting, and moments later the manbeast appeared with the morning paper in its mouth.

"Good boy," Michael cooed, patting the beast on the head and taking the paper. It nuzzled against his knee in response.

A headline caught Michael's eye. Something about shocked ramblers at Cromwell Bottom. The discovery of body parts. Thought to be a local woman. *'large scale enquiry…'* Blah blah blah, *'appealing to witnesses…'* Blah blah blah, *'Raped and murdered…'*

Well that was plain misrepresentation.

Shaking his head, he shuffled his way to the personal ads at the back of the paper and, taking a pen from the desk beside him, put a large black ring around 'Sandra, 36'.

Cairo Salutes

JOHN RATHBONE TAYLOR

HE FLINCHES WHEN he hears it. Outside, not far away, the barking and pining of a dog. Inside, he manages to remain silent, save for his troubled breathing and occasional grunts of pain.

He is in a wheelchair with a khaki sheet draped over his back and shoulders, like a cloak. He is wearing pyjamas with the seams of the sleeves and trouser legs cut to widen them. His left leg and foot are heavily bandaged, as are both his forearms and hands. He has gauze taped around and below the right side of his neck, and crepe bandage wound around his head, holding gauze across his forehead and eyebrows. Lighter bandaging and dressings cover his right ear and much of his face, with breathe-holes cut for his nostrils and mouth. His eyes are not covered. They can be seen clearly as he raises his head to listen and look in the direction of the unhappy animal.

His name is Harry Ackerson. His rank is Catering Sergeant. He has been wheeled in to the makeshift courtroom for this particular phase of questioning. Nurse Colette Durand stands at his side.

***

"... and range?"

"Six hundred twenty."

"Set six hundred."

"Rog' that! ... Six hundred ten, six hundred five, six hundred... and set!"

"On my command ... hold ... hold ... fi–"

The British tank-gunner fired, instinctively numbing his reflexes to the pulverising sound-shock of detonation. He let his body loosen – enough only to give himself into the Sherman's violent recoil.

The shell struck the oncoming Tiger tank, ripping off its right track and drive sprocket.

The German tank-gunner also fired, but half a second too late – just as the Tiger lurched sideways. Its cannon shell blasted off at an angle and buried itself in a sandbank two hundred yards away.

The Tiger couldn't be steered forwards or back. Its Commander screamed down to the gunner and driver:

"Reload! Reload! Rotate left thirty! Schnell! Schn–"

Before he could finish the order, a rocket from a swooping fighter plane blew the tank's turret away – and the top half of his body with it.

The ruptured rectangle of metal and flesh spun seventy yards through the air before it too slammed into the desert sand. The turret hit first, leaving the barrel pointing into the sky. To the British infantryman who watched it come down it looked ridiculous. Like some giant snorkel! But his attention was back on the decapitated Tiger. He was already calculating. Artillery fire and tank and airplane strafing was everywhere. More tanks and German infantry were coming. An ignored tank wreck could offer more protection and a better vantage point than his temporary trench-hole. No time for thinking twice about it. He grabbed the flame-thrower, hooped its feed tube over his shoulders and set off on a crouching run towards the smouldering vehicle.

Only yards from the Tiger, he stopped short. A severed human leg rose up from the top of the tank. It was being thrown. It arced into the air, bounced off the hull and fell to the ground before him. A second one was tossed after it.

A muscular figure with blood-streaked hair and a soot-covered face pushed himself up from the torn opening where the tank's turret had been. He clambered on to the flank of the hull and got to his feet, swaying as he did so. When he saw the infantryman he stilled himself and stared at the man, wide-eyed and unblinking. The whites of his eyes shone out against his blackened skin and the glistening red liquid trickling down his forehead. The infantryman saw only an expression of lunatic wildness. Calamity ran like a chill up his spine. His own eyes widened, and fear clenched his cheekbones. It didn't occur to him that this projected a similarly maniacal grimace to the German.

The two men gaped at one another until the German went to say something. He opened his left hand in an involuntary gesture as he did so. The infantryman immediately raised the flamethrower and shot off a venomous plume of fire at the man. Firing more in reaction than intent, his aim was not good. But the swirling tip of the flame-stream still reached and wrapped itself, whip-like, around the German's right ankle. It burned into his boot and gaiter on contact, and flared upwards along the thinner fabric of his trouser leg. He screamed as he tried to twist his upper body away from the fire swirl, and half-leapt, half-fell from the tank to the ground.

He landed awkwardly on his side. Straight away he threw up his free arm in a defensive gesture:

"Surrender! Surrender!" he shouted, "Please not shoot! Bitte! Take prisoner!"

Then he winced violently and turned to his burning trouser leg. He clenched his jacket cuff to the palm of his trailing hand and stabbed at the flames. He jerked around again and wailed at the infantryman.

"Bitte, bitte, Englisher, my leg is fire! Most pain! I am surrender. All my others dead. I am only loader man. Please to God help me!"

***

Tomorrow's flatbreads would be ready soon after midnight. Harry had laid out the dough pats, forty a-piece on each of the eight large baking trays, then loaded the trays into the catering unit's three big bread ovens. He'd been paddling bread and cake trays since before the war when he had his own bake-house, so the muscles on his left upper arm and right lower arm were noticeably developed in relation to the rest of him. He'd often get ragged about it if he walked around the camp in short sleeves.

"Been kneading the officers' bread Harry, or beating your monkey again?" they'd say. Or "Who've you been spanking this time, Acker, eh?"

Harry might chuckle to himself if anyone came up with an original jibe, otherwise he'd just huff and shake his head to let the pranksters know he thought their jokes corny. Sometimes, with the more stupid or thick-skinned ones he'd pretend to sneer and show them the finger.

In his presence, Harry's kitchen assistants never commented on his arm strength, or said anything else personal about him. They were POWs. They knew not to. He wouldn't expect it. He recognised all three of them were strong enough to lift a loaded tray on the oven paddle – especially POW Klaus Begemann, who had well-developed arm muscles also. But the POWs understood that lifting and balancing a paddle and loaded tray to chest level, manoeuvring them into a fire-hole without hitting the oven door, its side walls or the roof of the oven cavity, and doing this quickly enough to minimise heat loss – all took considerable skill. It was bakers' law in this kitchen that Sergeant Harry Ackerson trusted no-one but himself to do this thing. There was an occasion when he had delegated the job to Klaus – when Harry was off ill and had no alternative – and he did use Klaus to roll the dough pats; but otherwise, Klaus and POWs Rolf Ziegler and Gunter Hansen could do the other things.

After loading the ovens Harry had finished off the kitchen wash, scouring and rinsing the larger serving trays and cooking pans, the tureens and ladles. Now he was leaning back against the sink unit, drying his hands on his apron, and listening. The sounds of clunking wash-buckets and mopping in the store-room had ceased and the POWs were in conversation. Harry didn't understand German but he gathered from the tone and interplay of their voices that they were discussing a problem.

Rolf and Gunter seemed to be urging Klaus, their rank senior, to agree with them and to act in some way. The voices stopped, then Klaus stepped through the bead curtain doorway.

"My Rolf and Gunter have finished all things, and I too, mein Sergeant. But there is a place of hard grease and dirt upon the floor. Next to the stacking of cooking-oil drums and bully-beef tins. We cannot make this clean without I must ask you for more strong detergent."

Harry cursed under his breath. He'd been tipped off to expect an officers' spot inspection in the morning, so he'd already watered down what remained of his detergent ration for the extra cleaning. He needed everything tickety-boo, but he also wanted to finish early. This was the night he'd promised to take young Gunter into Cairo to see the belly-dancing. Though all three Germans had completed their stint in the store-room all the more enthusiastically, they were still tight on time. And time could be a problem. Disguising Gunter as one of the regular Tommies off to the 'entertainment' district for the evening would be easy enough. He'd done it with the others, and for the usual three ciggies, the supply-room Private had lent him the extra greatcoat and battalion beret he needed. That would get Gunter past the MPs. But if they were too late to walk out with all the other lads the gate sentry might spot something. It would need at least another four woodbines to buy his silence. No argument, they'd have to get this grease up, and pronto.

"Right Klaus, we need to do a hurry-up then. There's no 'strong' detergent. Tell Rolf and Gunter to dry these pans and ladles and put them away, and you mop this floor for me. Do it with water and vinegar. I'll see if I can scrounge some paraffin from the Transport lads. Be back in five minutes."

It took Harry nearer twenty minutes. Almost all the paraffin available had been commandeered by the outer defence units for their trench lamps. What was left had been securely locked in the Garage Sergeant's office for the night. Harry had to wait while the Garage Duty-Private syphoned a quarter-gallon of petrol from a senior officer's Jeep, in for a suspension repair. Two more ciggies and the promise of an extra chocolate ration.

When Harry returned he found the Germans seated round

the prepping table, partly-drunk mugs of tea in front of them. There was a full one waiting for Harry, at his empty chair. Klaus was leaning back on the other chair, smoking a roll-up. Rolf and Gunter were sat on upturned boxes, both perched forward with their elbows on the table. Gunter was noticeably red-faced, and he looked down at the floor when Harry came in. Rolf had his hands crossed and spread across his cheeks and mouth, but his eyes were laughing. With a covert wink and nod Klaus signalled to Harry that they'd been having fun with the youngster. Harry guessed they had been teasing him about what he was going to see that night. The lad was almost certainly still a virgin. Harry smiled knowingly at the two older men. Then he looked around the kitchen. He nodded a couple of times, gesturing and confirming his approval on seeing the freshly mopped floor. It looked spotless and already nearly dry. The electric fan had been brought in to help the warm, evening air circulate over the wetted surface.

"Good initiative, Klaus," he said, without looking back at the German.

Harry stood holding the fuel can, still eyeing up everything. He rubbed his chin with his free hand for a second before speaking:

"Tell Rolf to mix some more water and vinegar and have a go at cleaning the transom windows above the sink units."

Rolf heard his name and looked puzzled until Klaus translated for him, then he looked at the windows and nodded. Gunter knew some English, so he got up straight away when Harry suggested he should go fetch the overcoat and beret from the bunkhouse.

"Best if you're ready to go, lad, soon as we've topped this cleaning."

Gunter headed for the kitchen door. Rolf began to busy himself at the sink. Harry started towards the store room, gesturing to Klaus to come with him. Klaus pinched his roll-up, dropped forward off his chair and came with his limping gait around the table.

The German narrowed his eyes and shook his head to himself as he followed the Englishman and studied him from behind. He realised Harry had issued Gunter with the instruction to go the bunkhouse to allow the boy an escape from his embarrassment.

"Some day I will have to acknowledge this unassuming Englishman and his unexpected decency," he told himself. "This Sergeant Harry Ackerson is in charge of us because this is wartime and we are the Allies' captives. Yet, somehow, he never makes us feel anything less than his equals."

Klaus thought back to an incident six months earlier. Harry had been absent for two days, apparently with a nasty bout of 'Mummy's Tummy'. A Corporal from a different Catering unit had been assigned to oversee them. On Harry's return the man reported that he had seen Klaus feeding scraps to a scruffy-white terrier that hung around their kitchen block. Harry had looked displeased and told the Corporal he would deal with it, so Klaus had expected a scolding. But when the man had gone, Harry sat Klaus down, gave him a cigarette and thanked him for taking care of the dog. It turned out Harry had been secretly feeding the stray himself. He called the dog, 'Luckyboy'.

Klaus wondered what his parents in Freiburg would make of this tale when he was finally repatriated. Especially after their loss of the house, and the injuries his mother's sister had suffered, all as a result of British bombing. And what of the Brandt family, and the Krugers, whose boys, Willie and Michael, had died that grim death beside him when their Tiger had been hit? What would they say to Klaus, the only one to climb out of the pulverised panzer alive, if he was to tell them not just of the valour and sacrifice of their fine sons – the thing they would be so desperate to hear – but also of his positive experience in captivity from an enemy Englishman?

Inside the store-room Harry walked to where the oil drums and meat tins were stacked. He spotted what looked like the grease patch on the floor and pointed at it. Klaus nodded.

"It's probably leakage from the oil drums that's hardened over time," Harry said. "These tins don't always have perfect seams and the delivery blokes aren't that gentle with them. It should fetch up with this..."

He leaned forward and carefully poured some of the petrol

along the length of the patch. Then he stood up and produced two cleaning rags from his pocket. He tossed one to Klaus.

"You start that end. I'll start this."

Klaus knelt down and immediately smelled the petrol.

"This is not paraffin mein Sergeant. It is gasoline!" he said, concern in his voice.

"I couldn't get paraffin. But this'll do the job." Harry grinned and rocked his arm back and forth. "Come on Klaus, get that brawny arm moving!"

They both set to, rubbing away at the grease. It was softening, but the floor was rough concrete so their rags began to tear and it was difficult to get into its little indents and crevices. Harry leaned back, stretched himself and cricked his neck from side to side.

"Better fetch us some wire-wool, Klaus. And bring a couple of old pointed meat knives. I'll soften the stubborn bits with more petrol. We'll scrape and scour it. We can't do any more than that."

Harry mimed the arm movements again, this time overplaying the stabbing and prising actions.

Klaus laughed and said "Jawohl Herr Sergeant". He mocked a Nazi salute, purposely holding out his cleaning rag, dropping it, and imitating Harry's arm action as a clown's repeated, but failed attempts to catch the rag on its way to the ground. Harry laughed too. "Go! Schnell!" he said, pointing with his own rag at the store-room doorway. It was one of those moments when things clicked between them. Klaus pressed on his good knee to push himself up, then walked out of the store-room exaggerating his limp, knowing Harry would be tickled by his playfulness.

As Klaus picked two knives from the cutlery draw, Gunter came back in. The greatcoat was slung over his arm, but he was already wearing the battallion beret. Rolf noticed first and wolf-whistled. Klaus turned and was about to add a mickey-taking whistle himself when he heard a short squeak in the store-room, then a longer 'wroomp' sound that completely captured his attention. It was palpable, dull-noted and low-forming at first, but accelerating into a louder, dominating air gush that engulfed things. Klaus knew in an instant what it was, and in the next, he felt the horror coming. He became at once nauseated and breathless, and wavered off balance. He dropped the knives and swayed back against the metal work-top. His eyes rolled and the confusion started, but at the same time the 'help words' came to him. He didn't realise he was shouting them out loud in the kitchen:

"My hands! Get to my hands!"

He was already clenching his fists, forcing himself. He'd been here before and was getting practised. A part of him knew what to do now.

"The hands! The words and the hands!" he told himself. "The Me that moves them! Got to hold... hold on to the understanding. It's only a panicking mind. That isn't Me! I am the true... the one that does the understanding! Got to let the horror go. Let it pass. Mustn't hold it! Be alright then. Alright ... after the long second's passed."

In the other long seconds he'd been through, his hold on spatial reality, not only on his mind, always loosened. That was how the horror came. He knew he was about to go through it again, so he told himself again:

"Breathe Klaus, breathe in and let it pass you!"

The room had sentience but couldn't hold to its bearings. It lurched about, rising and plunging, zig-zagging its lights – everything meant to unbalance and dazzle him. It blurred its parameters and distances. He lost the sense of having things to hold on to. He was spinning between hallucinatory corners, doorways and shadows. Then everything suddenly in-folded. This was the shock point, the stomach-sickening moment when his trauma memory seized him and all self-volition would rush from him. He tried to focus on the breath he had just taken. His body convulsed as he did so...

...He was there again, trapped and choking in the blackness of the fume-filled, metal coffin... buried under bodies... his comrades' smouldering, torn-apart bodies!

...But something else was there. A voice he seemed to know about,

inside him, telling him that it was he that had air in his lungs, he whose fists were clenched. He who knew how to get out of this. He heard himself using the voice. It was He, Klaus.

"I move you now. Got to breathe, Willie! Forgive me, Michael, I get past you!"

As he spoke, Klaus looked down for his hands. He saw instead someone else's, on his forearms. Rolf's hands. And he realised Rolf was speaking at the same time as he was, saying something to calm him:

"... passed now, Klaus. You hear me, kamerad? It is over."

Barely had he grasped Rolf's words and realised his panic attack had passed – that he was breathing fully, back in control, aware of everything around him – than he was recalling and running over the sounds he had heard in the storeroom again. It was not a squeak, but a man's shriek he had heard, followed by a loud, ricocheting, clanging noise. It was Harry who had cried out. Then the other sound must have been the petrol-can Harry had been holding – crashing and bouncing on the store-room floor? But, it wasn't 'then' ... it was just now. Now!

Klaus raised his hands and smacked both of his cheeks. He looked up. Rolf and Gunter were standing together now, only feet away, staring at him with the same concern on their faces as he imagined was on his. The petrol-can exploded just as the three of them turned towards the store-room. The initial bang reverberated into a fracas of other violent sounds as flying metal struck ceiling and wall, glass shattered, and cooking oil burst from drums, ignited – and spattered a shower of fire over a screaming human. For Harry Ackerson was screaming – just as Klaus Begemann was shouting, and was swinging his gammy leg, loping towards the store-room as fast as he was able.

"Gunter, get help! Rolf, water!" he cried.

Burning fuel smoke and the smell of burning flesh hit Klaus as he entered the opening. His eyes smarted and he gagged, but he shouted for Harry. A gurgling cry came back. Klaus stepped blindly towards it. He made out a ray of light entering the room from a broken window. Smoke was curling up the beam. Harry was at the bottom of it, slumped on the floor with one leg stretched in front of him, the other bent awkwardly beneath him. His extended trouser leg, shirt front and sleeves were on fire. Smaller flames were spitting and streaking up the side of his face and around his ear, and part of his hair was smouldering. His eyebrows were black smudges below peeling skin, and his lips and nose a mess of red raw flesh, mucous and oil smears.

"Mein Sergeant," Klaus said, conscious immediately of how quietly he had spoken.

Harry groaned. His eyes were screwed shut but he lifted his face towards Klaus's voice and said, "Help ... me".

Klaus had on his cotton kitchen jacket. He ripped it off and smothered it around Harry's arms and upper body to starve the flames of oxygen. Using his forearm, he tried to do the same with the sizzling hair and skin around Harry's neck and ear, but Harry shrieked at the touch. Klaus spat two drools of saliva on the area instead. He turned to beating out the flames on Harry's trouser leg. Burning oil in the cloth stuck to the skin of his palm and fingers, but the pain brought the thought to him that this scorching was endurable compared to the searing-hot blast of a flame thrower, and he ignored it. He was worried though that he was starting to choke from smoke inhalation. He had to get Harry up, but how was he to do it? Just then the two of them were showered with a bucket of water! Rolf was behind him.

"Help me Rolf! Get the other side of him!" Klaus spluttered.

Harry howled as they hoisted him to his feet, but they managed to keep him conscious enough to put a little weight on to his less injured leg. This made it easier to steer him back to the kitchen. There they laid him carefully on the floor. Rolf made a pillow with a folded towel and slid it gently under Harry's head. When Gunter arrived with the Duty Officer, Klaus had just spread the borrowed greatcoat over Harry. He was leaning in close to Harry's face, telling him that the medics would soon be there to give him something for the pain.

***

The Officers' dining room had been re-organised for the inquiry. Divisional Commander Lesterly sat at the centre of the top table with one of his Lieutenants and the battalion Padre to one side of him, and the Major of the Medics' core on the other. Sub-Lieutenant Fenton of the Military Police was acting as court interrogator. Seats for Klaus, Rolf and Gunter were positioned in front of a side table. Only Klaus was standing. Due to his seniority of rank over the other two, and his better command of English, he was answering most of the questions.

"So, Lance-Corporal Begemann ..." said Fenton, avoiding the German titular rank name, 'Obergefreiter', that would credit Klaus with a slightly higher status. "We have heard from Corporal Jones, Duty Officer on the night in question, that after hearing an explosion in the catering unit and being alerted by POW Private Hansen, he rushed to the kitchen and found you and your other compatriot leaning over Sergeant Ackerson."

He passed a cursory glance at Rolf and Gunter.

"Corporal Jones also says that you were holding – no indeed – 'pressing' someone's greatcoat over Sergeant Taylor. Over his face as well as his body. I put it to you that you, Lance Corporal, saw and took the opportunity to murder Sergeant Ackerson, a man rightfully your superior, in rank, and in responsibility over you as a prisoner. You knew he was using petrol in the storeroom and you threw a match or a lighted cigarette on to the floor beside him to ignite it. This story of a spark from his army boot is pure invention. Who would believe such a thing?"

Fenton turned towards the Inquiry Commander and three officials alongside him. He raised his hand and made an exaggerated gesture of putting the tips of his thumb and index finger very nearly together:

"A tiny spark!" he said, with sarcasm.

Klaus was struggling to keep up with the speed of the Sub-Lieutenant's words and to comprehend the full meaning of what the man was saying. As he did begin to grasp the seriousness and implications of Fenton's accusations he turned pale and started to shake his head. Rolf and Gunter understood less of the interrogator's words but they had sensed the vindictiveness in his delivery. Now they could see the anxiety in Klaus's reaction. Rolf tapped Klaus's arm to ask what was wrong, but Klaus pushed his hand down without looking at him. Instead, he was trying imploringly to meet eyes with the Padre – whose own expression was almost as pained as Klaus's. Then quickly, he turned to look directly at Commander Lesterly:

"Nein... nein. No!" he shouted. "This is not true, mein Commandant!"

Fenton made to continue and the Commander rapped the table for order. The Padre leaned forward to say something to him but Lesterly raised a hand to stop him.

"No, Charles, please, wait a moment."

The Padre sat back in his seat, biting his lip. He exchanged pointed looks with the Major from the Medics' core, who also seemed uncomfortable.

Having gained the silence, the Commander addressed Klaus and then Fenton.

"Obergefreiter Begemann, you will keep your voice down if you please, and you will wait for Lieutenant Fenton to finish what he is putting to you. You will be given the chance to reply. Now, Lieutenant, say what you have to say if you will, but I believe it would be more fitting if you were to, to, let's say, slow down your delivery and moderate your tone a tad."

"Yes of course, Sir. I will try to do that, Sir," Fenton replied. He turned back to Klaus, and spoke his words slowly but firmly.

"I submit to you, Mister Begemann, that you thought you would get away with killing Sergeant Ackerson if you made it look like an accident. And further, I put it to you that when Sergeant Ackerson managed to drag himself out of the fire, you and those two men beside you tried to asphyxiate him. You thought we would conclude that the fumes from the fire killed him. You told POW Hansen to run off for help to fool us all into believing you. But when Corporal Jones turned out to be nearby, he appeared on the scene so quickly you were thwarted in your cowardly little game. And now you would have this Inquiry believe that you were trying to save Sergeant Ackerson..." Fenton paused then said, "...have us believe that you prisoners, 'German' prisoners... prisoners of war... act like heroes... towards your captors–"

Before Fenton could finish or Klaus could respond, the Padre spoke up. He looked indignantly at the Commander:

"I'm sorry Peter, Commander, but I must interject. I wish to put a question to Obergefreiter Begemann. Please do not make me insist on it."

Lesterly stared back at the Padre, at first without speaking – though his cheeks twitched. Then he nodded:

"Very well, Charles."

He signalled to Fenton to sit down for a moment. The Padre stood up. Klaus was still incensed, visibly trembling – struggling to hold his tongue and compose himself. The Padre took a few moments, then spoke:

"Obergefreiter Begemann, Klaus. I have only one question for you. It is really for all three of you. Please tell me honestly, what kind of a relationship did you have with Sergeant Ackerson?"

Klaus swallowed at the question. His breathing faltered with emotion; his chest rose and fell and he blinked away the tears that filled his eyes. Though he gave his answer to the Padre, as he spoke it, he turned to face Harry:

"He was… he is, our best friend."

Klaus stood to attention and saluted Harry. Rolf and Gunter immediately stood up from their seats and also came to attention. They too, saluted in Harry's direction.

No-one in the courtroom spoke, but everyone turned to look at Harry. He was staring across at Klaus and trying with difficulty to raise his bandaged right arm. The nurse understood what he wanted and placed both her hands under his arm as he raised it, as close as he was able to, into the soldiers' salute position.

Harry whispered something to the Nurse.

"Nurse Durand. Please repeat to the court what Sergeant Ackerson has just said to you," Commander Lesterly asked.

"He tells me, monsieur," she smiled, "He said we are both bakers!"

She

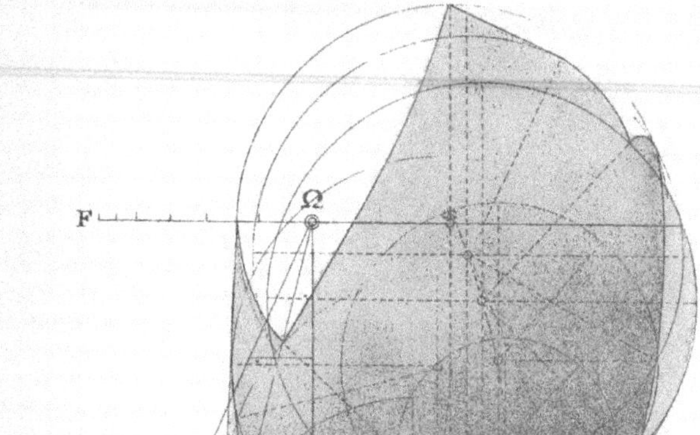

She 2

FORD DAGENHAM

she says she's probably got an ulcer
she says she always tastes her tears
and
she scrapes the ice and frost
out the top of the office fridge
to make a nothing slushy
and
i remember a winter when i saw her in the lift
with a fistful of snow
for lunch

A Greyhound Pass

ERINNA METTLER

SHE HAS WORKED as a waitress for as long as she can remember. It is all she knows how to be. Coffee flows through her veins, ketchup drives her heart, the smell of fried onions fires her brain.

Betty-Jo was just sixteen when Mr Simms built The Coyote Diner on the edge of town, where Main Street seamlessly transforms into Route 58. The town was small and perpetually covered with a thin layer of pale desert dust, as if it had been kept in storage for a long, long time. There was one bar on the outskirts, frequented by drunks and farm-hands, and no place for kids or women. The excitement amongst the bored backyard teenagers grew with the building site, as out-of-town workmen levelled the one-pump gas station and erected eatery Eden. The kids watched its progress from porches and push-bikes, standing in huddles to gawp at the passing trucks and rising walls and to speculate on how the place would look when it was finished. It was 1962, and those workmen left behind more than just a building; they left the tiny dirt-track town the much needed hope of rock 'n' roll glamour and more than one illegitimate child.

Betty-Jo went to see Mr Simms before the work was completed, the main shell having been constructed but the inside not yet beautified. She peered through the glass door, still with its protective plastic sheen, and watched him scan the local paper and slurp back coffee. He was a big, grey-haired Texan, complete with the requisite Stetson and spurs, even though his Chevrolet Impala was parked outside.

Men were a mystery to Betty-Jo. Her Daddy had left when she was nine – preferring hard liquor and gambling to providing for a family – and then it was just her and her Momma, who spent her life sitting silently on the porch in her rocking-chair mending the town's clothes for a meagre living. From this spot Betty-Jo's Momma squinted at the desert, which stretched out between the peaks that punctuated the town, as if she were waiting for somebody to ride over the horizon. Somebody she knew deep down would never come. Money was tight. Sometimes Betty-Jo dreamt of going to Vegas and winning big on the gaming tables she'd seen in the movies so that she and her Momma wouldn't want for anything. Whenever she mentioned this, her Momma would reply that money was better when it was earned and that Betty-Jo should concentrate on her studies instead of spending her time day-dreaming about things she'd never have. Betty-Jo never was one for schooling. Her Momma was right; she did spend most of her time in the classroom gazing out of the window, the teacher's words lost in the mist of her daydreams. She wouldn't ever be college material, but she had the savvy to walk up to The Coyote's door, before any of the other girls in town, and ask for a job. She stood a good while at that door before Mr Simms got the feeling he was being watched and spilled his coffee on himself as he started up and beckoned her in. As soon as she stepped over the threshold she knew she belonged.

In 1962 The Coyote seated a hundred and fifty. It had the smooth chrome lines of an express train complemented by deep, red, leather booths and bar stools. Each table had a mini jukebox, ensuring that the music was always on. When Betty-Jo arrived for her first day, in her short pink uniform and regulation lipstick, The Tornados blasted through the outdoor speakers and grease monkeys in newly pressed overalls tuned up cars on the parking lot. They stopped and whistled as she passed and she felt more like she was in an Elvis movie than starting work in her hometown.

In the back room, under a fog of competing perfume, the

girls fixed their make-up and hair for the grand opening. Betty-Jo knew a few of them – Cherry, Marlene – but mostly they were from out-of-town, and Betty-Jo blushed with pride when they complimented her on her legs as she tied the laces of her roller skates. They became the sisters she never had and Chet, the grill cook with movie-star looks, became her first husband, though none of them knew what they would mean to each other on that first day. Back then, they shared an unconscious immortality, certain only that the next day would be better than the last.

The Coyote's fame spread. The last stop before the desert, it drew customers from far and wide on their way to the natural wonders of the valley. It was also the place to hang out if you were young and looking for love. Betty-Jo was its star, a whizz on roller-skates, Mr Simms' favourite girl, popular with customers and co-workers alike. It was no wonder; she was very striking, tall and thin with the friendliest of ice-cream smiles. Her hair flowed in unruly auburn curls that kept coming loose from the bobby pins she used to keep them up. She considered it her best feature, even if it did smell of burger grease.

All that was nearly fifty years ago; and on almost every day of the intervening years – barring the few taken for funerals, childbirth and holidays – Betty-Jo has looked out across the parking lot to the desert at sunset. There is a particular moment she likes best, when dusk begins to dissolve into night and the sun tucks itself beneath the covers of the horizon. She always takes a minute to stand and watch its progress, awestruck as the orange light casts lengthening cactus shadows across the plain. The Coyote's vast windows give her the full Panavision experience. In these moments, she feels at one with the world. Today is the last day she will witness this spectacle as a waitress and she has a lump in her throat as she watches a lone car move slowly away toward the infinite.

From her first day at The Coyote, Betty-Jo remembered everybody's name. It came naturally to her, as if the brainpower needed to retain all the arithmetic and fancy words in school was just waiting for a purpose. She added up cheques in her head and remembered the favourite dishes of her customers, even if they had only visited once or twice. If folks were new to town she greeted them warmly as they settled into a booth and made sure to ask how they were doing. Sometimes it was hard. Sometimes her heart felt like it would break. In her time at The Coyote, she has gone through two husbands and her fair share of lovers. Chet ran off with another waitress after ten years together. Her second husband, a refined older man named Mitch, died of lung cancer a few years after they wed. Both left her a son apiece, Eddie and little Malcolm. Even when they were babies she managed to work full time, night shifts and afternoons, leaving them with their grandma until they were old enough for school. Later, they came to the diner after class and Mr Simms always gave them a jawbreaker while they picked something from the menu for supper and did their homework in the back room. Mr Simms was a sympathetic boss, more like a granddaddy to her boys. He said they were as cute as pie with their mother's red hair and Opie freckles and he taught them their first magic tricks, and then poker, over the counter as Betty-Jo worked.

Malcolm was killed in Iraq. He was twenty-nine. They flew him home in a coffin wrapped in the stars and stripes. The army presented her with the flag at the funeral. A young man with a straight back and a square jaw placed it on her upturned hands and then saluted her. She had no tears left to cry. She keeps Malcolm's flag folded in her dresser drawer, out of sight but never quite out of mind.

Eddie didn't cope too well. He got deep into drugs, and the crimes that go with them, and ended up with a fifteen year prison sentence for armed robbery. Neither son had married. There are no grand-kiddies to dote on, not yet, and not without considerable luck. Eddie isn't young anymore; his red hair was shaved to the skin last time she visited and his face was puffy and grey. Betty-Jo wishes she could visit him more often but he's in a cross-state penitentiary and the bus fare is more than she can afford. That's her business though. The customers don't need to know about her personal dramas. For them, she has only a smile and a few words of encouragement when it looks like they might be suffering.

In the 1970s the music changed. Approaching thirty, Betty-Jo adapted her roller-skating technique, swishing in time to heavy disco beats with a tray poised preternaturally on one hand. The diner still buzzed and Betty-Jo still wore her smile. Most of the original Coyote girls had left, married or gone South to seek fame and fortune. Betty-Jo was older than the new girls and more like a mother than a sister. She gave them advice when they had man-trouble – God knows she'd had enough herself – and provided a shoulder to cry on when they needed it. Mr Simms looked after her, made sure she was eating right and had enough shifts to pay the rent. She thought of him as the father she never had, a bond unspoken but acknowledged in the cheery *'mornin, how are you?'* they exchanged each day. When Betty-Jo's momma passed he paid for the funeral and afterwards sat with her until dawn sharing bourbon and memories.

Another decade passed under the unforgiving desert sun and Betty-Jo's skin began to wrinkle. She had good genes but the laughter lines ran deep turning her mouth down at the edges so, unless she was fully smiling, she carried an air of sadness about her. She still loved her job, though it wasn't the same after Mr Simms had his heart attack. Right there in the spot she'd first seen him, almost thirty years to the day. He slumped to the floor and his coffee spilled on the table, seeping into his newspaper and blurring all the stories into one. The Coyote passed to a nephew, who never came near, and the management of the place was taken over by a young man called Gregory, who had a sour face and a silent manner. A Starbucks opened on Main Street and a drive-thru McDonald's across the road. People wanted their food fast. Custom dwindled quickly and within a year of Mr Simms death half of the booth space in The Coyote was given over to slot machines. The music was turned way down.

Today, Betty-Jo shows her replacement the ropes. Carmine is her name; it doesn't suit her. She is a tiny, mousy thing with glasses and acne, just out of school. She has to be shown how the staff lockers work several times; God knows how she'll cope out front, but that's not Betty-Jo's problem anymore. At least the roller-skates have long been replaced by sensible sneakers, rubber-soled so as not to mark the floor. As Carmine stows her outdoor shoes in her locker, Betty-Jo looks at herself in the back room mirror. She smoothes her hands over her belly, noting how her uniform stretches across her bulging middle, and then touches the tight grey perm peeking from under her hat. The auburn curls are gone. For some time now she has been squinting at her order pad through bi-focal lenses. Her smile is the same though, a little puckered around the edges maybe, but still as radiant as a desert morning.

Betty-Jo's last order is a rush. At six-thirty the door is opened by a stranger wearing blue jeans and a pressed white shirt. She saw his pick up drive in from the valley, sunlight reflecting off the wing mirrors like fallen stars. It's unusual to see an unfamiliar face at The Coyote these days. He carries a Stetson and, though he bears no physical resemblance to Mr Simms (he's too short and dark), he reminds Betty-Jo a great deal of her former boss; perhaps it's his soft Texan accent and twinkling eyes. He orders coffee and blueberry pancakes with canned cream and as she pours Betty-Jo asks on the off chance if he is related to Mr Simms. *Wouldn't that be something on my last day?* She says. But the stranger smiles and tells her he's just passing through and there's no connection at all. Betty-Jo is as attentive as ever but her co-workers spring a Happy Retirement cake on her so she doesn't have as much time to talk to him as she would like. Gregory – now middle-aged but no more communicative – makes a short embarrassed speech about her being their longest serving employee. There is applause and tears and they present her with their gift – a china model of a cowgirl riding bare-back. It's pretty, hand-painted, with fine detail on the long red curls sticking out under the cowgirl's hat. Perhaps they thought it looked like she did in the old photographs that now adorn The Coyote's walls. It's a lovely gift, planned, thoughtful and completely useless. Betty-Jo hides her disappointment under her usual enormous smile. A Greyhound pass was what she wanted, so she could visit Eddie more often. She was sure she had dropped enough hints.

After the party, she places her cowgirl safely under the counter and insists on clearing her last table. The Texan is long gone. He smiled and tipped his hat to her during the celebrations. She watched him walk to his car as the waitresses set off party poppers and sang 'For She's A Jolly Good Fellow'. Betty-Jo pockets his tip without looking at it, assuming from his smile that it is a more than generous note. She goes out for a farewell beer with her colleagues, knowing she will see them rarely. She doesn't think she could bear to come back as a customer. The Coyote is as much her diner as it is anyone's; it wouldn't be right to be waited on. It is only when she is home, sitting alone in front of the TV rubbing her stockinged feet, that she remembers the tip. She sits up and fishes into her coverall pocket. She is surprised to find that the folded paper in her palm isn't the twenty dollar bill she was expecting but a lottery ticket for that night's county draw. She thinks about her momma, sitting on the porch mending clothes, telling her that money is better when it's earned. Betty-Jo remembers her teenage dream of winning big in Vegas, a city her momma never got to visit. A smile crosses her lips as she reaches for the TV remote and changes the channel just in time to catch the jackpot draw.

No Regrets

GORDON WILLIAMS

SHE WAS SURROUNDED by faces but only interested in her own. A silent audience of black and white photographs – previous occupants of this room, the nearly famous and the forgotten – looked on as she applied her make-up. Three hours at the hairdresser's that afternoon had changed her grey roots to the same auburn colour as the rest of her hair, now set in mid-length curls. Blusher completed, she applied eye shadow and mascara as intermittent laughter rose in distant muffled waves beyond the room. She brought her face closer to the mirror to confirm she had finished her lashes, put the little black brush back in its case on the dressing table and picked up her lipstick as another wave of laughter broke past the corridor outside the door. A pout, some heightened local redness, another pout and a tissue gently pressed between her glistening lips. There was more laughter, music starting and people clapping. Sideways on, left and right, she nodded in agreement with the face looking back.

A last look as the music and applause faded away. She stood and did a half-twirl to each side, admiring the reflection of her glittering gold strapless dress as it sparkled, lit by the circle of pink lights surrounding the mirror, before holding the dress with both hands behind her to ease herself into the brown leather armchair. She switched off the lights around the mirror but the harshness of the fluorescent ceiling light left the small room, with its windowless magnolia walls and brown carpet, looking as ordinary as it was, so she switched the mirror lights back on and put her tights-clad feet up on the dressing table.

Resting her hands on the cigarette-burned arms of the armchair, she closed her eyes and took a deep breath in.

Before she could breathe out somebody knocked at the door and said, "Debbie?"

She opened her eyes and asked, "Who's that?"

"Tommy. Tommy Nash," the voice answered in a thick Scouse accent.

She said, "Shit," quietly to herself, took her feet off the dressing table and went to the door, where her black cashmere coat hung on a hook. She unlocked the door and saw a tall, overweight man, with thin hair greying at the sides, grinning and taking up most of the doorway.

He wore a dark suit with a purple bow tie and asked, "How's it goin', kid?"

"No better for seeing you," she answered, and walked back to her chair as Tommy followed her.

"I saw your name on the bill and thought I hadn't seen much of you recently," Tommy said, "although in that dress I'm not sure."

"How did it go tonight?" Debbie asked as she sat down beside her mirror.

Tommy bent forward to unfasten his bow tie and top shirt button.

"Gorra few laughs," he replied. "Nobody threw anything. The usual Friday night crowd. I haven't been here for a while but at least they asked me back. When was you here last?"

"Before Christmas," said Debbie. "I usually go down well here. Do the songs they all know. Keep 'em happy."

She leaned over the arm of her chair and pointed to the room's other chair – black leatherette, torn at both top corners – by the door.

"Sit down," she told her guest. "I'm on after the bingo so I've got nothing to do for twenty minutes. Even talking to you's better than sitting here on my own."

"Thanks, kid. It's great to feel wanted," Tommy said, rolling his bow tie around his hand and stuffing it in his jacket pocket.

"Sorry, Tommy, but it's been a bad week," Debbie said.

"I wondered why you had a face like a smacked arse,"

Tommy said as he sat down. "So what's happened then? House repossessed? World War Three? Got pregnant?"

"No, you silly bugger. Did you see *The Des O'Connor Show* on Tuesday?"

"No... er, Tuesday... I was doing a stag night in Preston. I did the bluest stuff I know and it went down great."

"You don't usually do really blue stuff..."

"I give 'em what they want, like you do. I couldn't get away with that here but I was bluer than an Eskimo's varicose veins last Tuesday – they were so pissed they'd have laughed at anything. So what was wrong with Des O'Connor? I've watched him meself sometimes but he's never spoiled my week."

"It wasn't Des," Debbie replied, leaning back into the armchair. "That bastard Marty Mann was on his show. I'd hoped I'd never see his face again, even if it did look like it had been ironed. He must have had those Botox injections. And his hair was darker than when I last saw him – and that was over twenty years ago."

"Who's Marty Mann? I've never heard of him."

"I wish I'd never heard of him. We used to be in a band together a long time ago, called Daybreak..."

"I remember them – I must have been in short pants at the time..."

"Well they must have been bloody tight on you, 'cos you're about the same age as me."

"How old's that, then?"

"Thirty-nine. Just like my mother: she was thirty-nine for so long I eventually overtook her."

"Well if you knew this fella over twenty years ago, you must have been..."

"A child star, like Shirley Temple," Debbie interrupted.

"So what's happenin' with this Marty fella?" Tommy changed the subject.

"He's come back to Britain for a tour and to promote his new CD."

"What's wrong with that?" Tommy asked.

"He said on Des's show that he was hoping to re-form

Daybreak. That was the first I'd heard about it and I was the lead singer. He never asked me."

"It could be worth a few quid if they re-form. Better than singing in places like this," said Tommy as he waved his arm about. "What's the problem?"

"That two-faced creep Marty's the problem. All the trouble he caused when we split up. He cleared off to Australia while the rest of us had to work to pay off the contract we were stuck with. I'd never heard of him for years but they said he'd made a name for himself there..."

"Is he big Down Under?" said Tommy.

"I could tell you... but so could a lot of women. I should have known better," Debbie shook her head, her auburn curls swinging. "When we first started we spent three years driving around in a Transit, playing every crummy gig we could get before we got signed up by a record company. Marty could play guitar OK but he wasn't much of a singer. And he was great at hustling. That and chasing women. He managed to combine business and pleasure by charming the knickers off a PA to some record company boss to get us an audition. When they signed us it was like Christmas every day: three hit records, an album, concerts – we were on *Top of the Pops* four times..."

"I must have seen yer – in me short pants an' all..."

"...interviews, meeting famous people – I actually met Shirley Bassey and Cliff Richard. I was on cloud nine for eighteen months. Then it all ended," Debbie said through her teeth.

"How come?"

"Marty and me had been an item for over a year. It was the best year of my life – everything was going so well. We rented a house in the country where nobody knew us – it would have been bad for the image if Marty had a girlfriend or a wife. Only those in the band knew about me and Marty. I thought I was the one to stop him wandering... but I was wrong."

"What was he up to?"

"I found him with one of our backing singers before a gig in Leeds. And she was supposed to be going out with Tony, our drummer. They were in the dressing room but they were using it like the undressing room. I was hitting Marty with my handbag, then Tony heard the row and came in, and he started hitting him as well. And Marty's still trying to get his clothes on..."

"I wish I'd been there..."

"I wish I hadn't. We still had to do the gig that night. I had to sing a duet with Marty ... called 'Forever True'... "

"I remember it," Tommy started singing. *"All my life I'll spend with you – 'cos I'll be forever true..."*

"Stick to telling jokes, Tommy. I was singing three feet away from Marty – I could see his bruises from there, even under his make-up. I had to smile and sing through gritted teeth for an hour. I still sounded better than you. I heard there was another fight in the dressing room afterwards, but I'd already cleared off by then. It was in the papers two days later. I still remember the headline: *Daybreak Up."*

"So it all ended – just like that?" Tommy asked.

"Our manager tried to get us back together, telling us we still had six months of our contract to run but there was no chance: Jeff, our bass player, went into rehab for his coke habit and Tony ended up in detox in Withington. All the problems we'd been trying to hide caught up with us. When the papers found out there was another headline: *Daybreak Down."*

"So you had musical and personal differences, then?"

"You could say that. We only talked to each other through lawyers afterwards and I haven't seen any of the band for years – not till I saw Marty on the telly last Tuesday."

"What happened to all the money you made from the records and the concerts and that?"

"I wish I knew. The record company wouldn't pay us, saying we'd breached our contract. I got a lawyer to look at it; he said it was an unusual contract and we should have had somebody check it over before we signed it. That's how naïve we all were then – we were over the moon just to get a record deal. And our manager said we owed him money 'cos the rest of the tour was cancelled. I spent two years doing gigs in pubs and clubs – anywhere – to get enough money together to pay off what they said I owed. They were the worst gigs I ever did – singing to the sound of knives and forks scraping on plates because people were more interested in eating than listening to me..."

"I know, I've done it. I bet you've never played to an empty club like I did once: some place near Chester. I asked the manager if there was any point in going on and he said I wouldn't get paid if I didn't. So I did an hour in this empty club telling jokes to candles flickering on the tables. Didn't get many laughs that night."

"I've played some real dives myself but I've always had a few people in the audience. I was still calling myself *The Voice of Daybreak* then, even though I hated it, because it was the only way I could get any gigs. Since then I've kept quiet about it. Marty didn't bother trying to pay off what he owed – he just declared himself bankrupt and scarpered to Australia, the spineless little shit..."

"So you're not bitter about it then?" said Tommy.

"I didn't think I was till I saw him on telly the other night. All the trouble he caused and then he just ran away. And now he wants us to make up and be friends again." Debbie shook her head, and curls, again.

"So what's wrong with doing it just for the money?"

"I don't do this for the money now. I do it because I want to do it. I didn't bother while the kids were growing up but I had to start again a few years ago. Singing while I was doing the ironing wasn't enough. I had to be out there," she pointed at the door, "singing."

"You must've married a rich fella if you could stay at home all that time."

"I went to see an accountant to help me sort out the money problems after Daybreak finished – the tax and the contractual obligations. It was good to meet somebody normal for a change. Then I married him."

"I've got the same accountant as Ken Dodd," said Tommy. "He recommended him to me. Before that I thought because I lived on the coast in Southport I didn't have to pay money to the Inland Revenue."

"The old ones are the best, Tommy."

"There's always someone who hasn't heard 'em, thank God. You know they brought in self-assessment a few years ago? I thought of it long before they did. The accountant said he'd save me a lorra time – about two years if I got caught."

Debbie smiled for the first time that night, stood up and twirled.

"What do you think of my dress?"

"A bit smart for this place, innit?"

"It's one of Shirley Bassey's." Debbie twirled again and sat down, easing her dress into her chair with both hands. "Dave bought it for me at an auction. He wouldn't tell me what it cost but it'll end up as an allowable expense. I put it on tonight to cheer myself up." She pointed to the clock on the wall and said, "I'm on in five minutes."

"Go out there and slay 'em, kid. Don't let this Marty fella get to yer."

"His agent 'phoned me yesterday. Some smooth-talking Southerner. Asked me if I'd seen Marty on the telly. Said he was doing a comeback UK tour, and there'd been a lot of interest in the possibility of Daybreak reforming and doing a tour and a CD. The other members of the band had already agreed and they wanted me to consider it."

"So what did you say?"

"I let him keep talking. And when he told me how much they'd pay me I couldn't say anything because my mouth was still wide open."

"How much was that?"

"Enough for me and Dave to retire on. The agent fella kept talking and asked me if I'd heard Marty's new CD. I told him in Marty's case it stood for Compact Dick and there was more chance of John Lennon re-forming The Beatles than there was of me ever singing with Marty again. Then I cut him off and I've heard nothing from him since."

"Was that a wise career move?" Tommy asked.

"I don't care. No amount of money would make me go near that two-timing bastard again. He's just a third-rate singer who ruined things for me and everybody else."

"And he's on the telly and you're singing in Salford. Couldn't you call his agent back and say you've reconsidered?"

"I'd rather be mixing with the likes of strippers and drag

artists and you and all the other comedians you meet in this business than have to see Marty again."

"You could be right, kid," said Tommy. "There's worse things than doing this for a living – I know, 'cos I've done 'em. After fourteen years on the assembly line at Ford's I wake up every morning – and some afternoons – and thank God I'm still in this business. I might not be Billy Connolly but even dyin' on your arse in Burnley beats shift work at Halewood."

Debbie turned and took a mouthful of water from a glass on the dressing table, stood up to gargle and spat into the hand basin to her right. She bent towards the mirror to apply a final touch of lipstick, then climbed into her sparkling gold high heels.

"You've still gorra face like a smacked arse," Tommy said, standing up. "Go on – give us a smile, kid."

Debbie pulled a face in reply.

"I suppose a fuck's out of the question then tonight?" Tommy asked.

"Sod off. I'm on in two minutes."

"That's all I need some nights."

"You're still the same, Tommy. And so are the jokes. Sorry, but it's show time… and tonight I'm going to be… Shirley Bassey. Again."

"Go on, kid – break a leg," said Tommy as he stood up.

"I'll break yours if you don't get out of my way," Debbie said and walked to the door.

Tommy followed her through and waited as she locked the dark blue door with its shiny yellow star stuck on above the words *Artiste's Dressing Room* and bent to put the key in her shoe. They walked along the corridor of cream-painted brick walls decorated with more framed black-and-white photographs towards the sound of voices at the side of the stage where the bingo prizes were being given out. Tommy told her to break her other leg as she took several deep breaths and waited. The compere, thin and balding in a charcoal suit, frilly shirt and lilac bow tie, gave out the last of the prizes and walked offstage to greet her.

"Hiya, darlin'," he said as leaned forward to kiss Debbie's cheek, close enough for her to smell the lager on his breath and feel his moustache tickling her skin. "You in good form?" he asked. "The place is full and they're ready for you."

Debbie tried to smile; she didn't speak but kept on taking slow, deep breaths as the compere walked back to the microphone at the centre of the stage. The house lights went down and the footlights brightened to show cigarette smoke curling upwards around the compere's legs.

"Ladies and gentlemen," the compere began, "we're always very pleased to invite this lady to our club. She's a fabulous singer and a great favourite of ours, so please give a big welcome to... Debbie Clarke."

The band – three middle-aged men in dinner jackets squeezed onto the left hand side of the stage with their guitar, organ and drums – starts into 'Hey, Big Spender' and she walks onstage to lively applause.

"Good evening ladies and gentlemen," she tells them as the intro fades, "it's always good to be back here. I'm going to start this evening with a song you all know – 'Memory' from *Cats*."

Streisand may do it better but she never played Salford Labour Club. It's as good a version as they've heard here, followed by 'I Will Always Love You', with notes as long as Whitney ever held. The applause allows her to pause for breath, then she waits for two men carrying trays of drinks from the bar to reach their table near the front. The spotlight makes her gold dress sparkle and stand out from the burgundy curtain behind her. She lifts the microphone from its stand and starts into 'Cry Me A River', deep and heartfelt, walking slowly across the stage. The guitarist takes his solo and she looks out at the audience – four rows of crowded tables stretching away from the stage to the bar at the back – before rejoining the band for the last verse. When they finish clapping she tells them:

"This is the most beautiful love song ever written by somebody from Salford... or anywhere else for that matter," introducing Ewan McColl's 'The First Time Ever I Saw Your Face'. The respectful silence holds between its slow lyrics as nobody dares to lift a glass and spoil the effect.

When the applause subsides she does a twirl, asks:

"Do you like the dress?" and gets several wolf whistles in

reply. "It's one of Shirley Bassey's that my husband bought for me. I've always wanted one." Then she leans towards the organist and tells him, "I bet you've always wanted to get into one of Shirley's dresses." When they finish laughing she tells her audience, "This is one of Shirley's dresses and this... is one of her songs," launching into 'As Long As He Needs Me' with full dramatic effect, leading to a climax that demands applause.

"Do you want some more of Shirley's songs?" she asks when the clapping ends.

Without waiting for a reply she nods to the band, who start their intro to 'Hey, Big Spender' and she gives it everything, shaking Shirley's dress and its contents before leaning suggestively over two startled men at a table near the stage. Their wives are laughing and the applause allows her to take some more deep breaths before launching into 'What Kind Of Fool Am I?', slowing the tempo again to prepare herself for the full-on vocal assault of 'I Who Have Nothing'. The applause gets louder and some of the audience are cheering.

She takes another bow and announces, "Ladies and gentlemen – thank you for being such a lovely audience. I'm going to finish off this evening with a song made famous by a woman that the French called *The Little Sparrow*, but I'm going to do the version that Shirley did a long time ago – in English, because I don't speak French and I know that not many people in Salford do, either. Edith Piaf was tiny and she wasn't good-looking, but she lived life as it's meant to be lived – to the full. This is 'No Regrets'."

A short intro and straight in... *No, no regrets*... the warbled phrasing just like Piaf's, even without the French accent ...*No, we will have no regrets* ... that strength and that vulnerability as she dominates each verse, each chorus... *One last kiss, shrug and sigh*... she gives it everything and they're transfixed by the intensity that she generates... *No regrets.... even though it's... good... bye.*

A stepped crescendo that stretches her voice to its triumphant limits. The big finish and then some. The applause surrounds her and continues for long enough to demand an encore, as she stands bowing in the spotlight, catching her breath and hoping that the tears and mascara running down both cheeks haven't spoiled her finale.

For My Sins

MAX DUNBAR

SHE HADN'T SEEN this coming. She had expected someone gaunt and grave.

The sin-eater was a fat man with curly, almost bouffant grey hair that made Lexi think of Donald Trump. He wore a bomber jacket and denim shirt that carried stains from long-ago meals, faded into the fabric like patchwork. When he spoke, Lexi saw that his teeth were bent and croggled.

"Miss Blythe, is that right?" The sin-eater pushed past without waiting for an answer. He didn't bother either to take off his boots or to wipe them, and messy footprints appeared on the hall carpet as he strode. "Can I trouble you for a cuppa?"

"Yeah," Lexi said following him, a woman with a soft face and a good body, billowing hair and sharp eyes. She brewed coffee and took two mugs out to where the sin-eater sat in slants of sunlight from the French doors looking out onto the garden. The mugs had CHROMOSAL TEC logos on them.

"Fucking good view up here," the sin-eater remarked. "Can see right downt' Abbey."

"It's great for parties when summer comes," Lexi said. "So, can we get to the point? How does this work exactly?"

She wanted to move things on: the sin-eater had the style of a man who would talk away the afternoon about nothing. And she was tired.

"Did Mr Day not tell you anything? Terrible remiss of him. Still, he ain't a reliable man. Sold a bunch of bad pills that killed his best friend at Global Gathering. Police never traced it back to him, of course, but it's *the dark night of the soul* that gets you, don't you find that, Miss Blythe?" The sin-eater had a giggly, rollicking voice that was out of sync with the morbid nature of his words. "Terrible guilt that young man went through. Mr Day almost took the jump, did he tell you that? OD'd, had to have his stomach pumped at the LGI. Terrible. Still, I got to him in time, and now he's fine."

"He didn't tell me any of that. We were talking at a party, he just recommended you. He didn't tell me what the treatment actually involves. Are you like an alternative health guy?"

When the sin-eater talked his teeth waggled like piano keys.

"Nah, I ain't new age. I been around a long long time, before Jesus even. This ain't about reflexology or sticking pins in your head or paying fifty quid for a bottle of water. This is serious shit, Miss Blythe." The sin-eater drank down half his coffee as if it were water. "You need to tell me everything. And I mean everything. *Feed me.* It's pretty intense, I warn you. I seen grown men crying over this."

"I just want the guilt to end," Lexi said. "I want to be able to wake up without feeling afraid and to sleep through the night. I have my house, my money, my social life, I should be able to enjoy all that without the guilt."

"Once you've given your full account, you take a little blood from your hand – no way around this, I'm afraid, so it's tough luck if you're squeamish – and mix it into the food you're gonna prepare for me."

"Does it have to be a particular kind of food?"

"Nope." The sin-eater tossed back the rest of his coffee. "Can be anything. But I like burgers."

Lexi grew up on the Hawkswood estate. Her best friend was a girl called Kelly Dales. As teenagers they wagged off school, got drunk down at the Aire with the popular crowd, sledged on Toboggan Hill when it snowed, and did everything they could to fight the atmosphere of tedium and bitterness that pervaded the Hawk. Kelly's passion was computers. She could make little arcade games and personal websites, and showed Lexi how. By the time they were fifteen both girls could code to industry standard. They used this talent to hack into the school computers so that they all crashed at the beginning of the lesson, displaying an error message that read '404 Error: Mr Schofield bends it'.

When Mr Schofield found out what Lexi and Kelly had done, he did not punish them as they had expected. Mr Schofield asked them how they had done the coding. Mr Schofield got very excited and started talking about algorithms and systems and domains. He said that when they left school they should go to college and do a degree in programming. Then they could get jobs at Google or Microsoft. There was loads of money in computers, he said.

Mr Schofield mentioned this at parents' evening, and Lexi's mam just laughed and said that college would be too expensive, and who was going to pay for it, and that sort of thing wasn't for the likes of them anyway. Lexi knew what she meant. You didn't go to college. You left school at sixteen and had a baby and got a council house and maybe a part time job as a nursery nurse or care assistant. That was the algorithm of the Hawk.

Lexi hardly ever ate burgers and had made the sin-eater's meal out of a breakfast muffin and leftover mince from the shepherd's pie *dauphinoise* recipe she'd served to guests last weekend. The burger didn't look nice to eat.

"Is it me or is this thing *pul*sating?" she asked.

"That's your sin."

He sprayed ketchup, mustard and mayo, one after the other, on top of the throbbing meat, then demolished the patty in five minutes. The sin-eater then downed half a San Pellegrino and produced a belch like God's death-rattle.

"Much obliged. That was delish."

"How much do I owe you?"

The sin-eater got to his feet, wiping his mouth with his sleeve.

"Fuck all. That's how you can tell I ain't an alt-health practitioner. It's the pain and regret and misery I like to eat, for each sin's a drop of honey to me."

Actually she'd felt nothing while she told the tale. Even enjoyed the retelling. Thinking about Kelly had been worse than talking about her. For after school let out for the last time Kelly and Lexi spent a few years working minimum wage and getting wrecked in the Bridge or LS6. Then they discovered webcamming. For a floor show lasting maybe three hours, they could clear three hundred each, even after the camsite had taken its cut. It was fun, they had their regulars and a real sense of community to the whole thing, people used to tip big when their shih tzu dog, Barney made an appearance, or when they could see Kelly's older brother watching at the door.

Lexi's mam found out about the webcamming and kicked her out, but by then they were making enough to rent a decent flat up by Beckett Park anyway. They had lunches in town and bought cool clothes and went to parties. But Kelly was not satisfied. She had always been the more ambitious and accomplished of the two, and was working on what she called a 'killer app' – something that everyone with a smartphone would want. At the same time she started going out with a lad named Pete Forrester, a big shot who worked as a web developer in the city's financial district. Lexi thought this was slightly unfair – she had met Pete Forrester first, had got off with him at Vanessa Rideout's New Year's Eve party in the hills. But aside from flirting and cockteasing Forrester when Kelly wasn't around, there was nothing she could do.

Last year Kelly had finished the app: a free game called 'Eat the Bean'. You played a cute little dinosaur that had to run around the place, eating beans that fell from the sky. The thing was ridiculously addictive, and Kelly started sending samples out to software companies. The way Lexi told it, the screentime had burned itself into her face so that Kelly had looked rough for a while, and she'd developed an awful rattly cough, even though she'd never smoked. Last summer Kelly had started to cough all the time. Then Kelly started to vomit. Then Kelly started vomiting blood. It was scary. Lexi thought she might have cancer. It wasn't cancer, though. It was something called *idiopathic pulmonary fibrosis,* and over the next six months it went about the business of killing her.

After the sin-eater had gone she went to lie down for a while, but found she couldn't get to sleep. Her heart seemed to dance with playful emotions, and marvellous universes formed and collapsed behind her eyes. She wondered why she was even in the house on such a sunny day. She went for a run around the Abbey and then hit the Clock Cafe for a beer and some nachos. The sun was out late and she wandered over to the Bridge Inn.

Most of Lexi's and Kelly's friends had been students or post-graduates or people just out of uni and casting around for some big idea. There were plenty of the old crew in the beer garden.

"Jesus, looks like we might actually get a proper summer this year!" Johan said. "It's like the bloody Strongbow advert."

"Lex," Day said, "got any holidays planned?"

"We should go to Benidorm," Fran said. "Lexi! Let's do ironic Benidorm!"

"Nah," Lexi said. "Benidorm is not good even in an ironic way. I only holiday in places with an umlaut."

They ended up at a little session at Johan's place: a session that turned into a party. She remembered lying in an attic next to Fran, and bars of strobes coming through the spaces between the beams, and the beat of something – Faithless' 'Insomnia' – pulsed in and out with the lights.

"Lexi," Fran said, "you look great. For the first time in months."

Lexi knew this. Everyone had been telling her. Day had that energised unburdened look, too.

What she said was: "I *feel* great."

"I can tell. And it's good to have you back. We thought, you know, you kind of blamed yourself for what happened to Kelly."

"Maybe I did," Lexi said. "Maybe it was, like, survivor's guilt."

"Did your therapist tell you that?"

"Yes," she said, lying. Her therapist had referred her on after she'd offered him oral sex in return for codeine drugs. "It can be good. Traditional therapy. Old school."

Over the next weeks she wondered really what she had made so much fuss about. It had maybe been the stress of looking after Kelly that had fucked her up. She hadn't had to work; the app money had come through, and most of the time after buying the house she had simply lain around in it, entire days watching Netflix and reading fashionista blogs and eating takeaway, sometimes going to an event she couldn't possibly avoid or calling up an old friend with benefits for the evening. She remembered so much of the time she wanted to sleep because asleep you didn't feel the *wrongness* of yourself like a pickaxe in your chest. She had eaten a lot of chocolate, she recalled, or at least watched a lot of chocolate commercials – commercials that pitched breathless clichés of *desire* and *indulgence* and *sin*.

But now that she was up and about and socialising again, cleaning the house and buying new clothes and back on the LS6 party scene, she thought that maybe she had been too harsh on herself. After all, she had looked after Kelly for six long months. A dreary whirlwind of appointments and bureaucracy and care packages and adaptations. Of seizures and night terrors and fingers turning blue. Lexi hadn't ever had to look after a sick person before, and she was fire fighting. *The reason I moved out after the deal came through,* Lexi had told the sin-eater, *is not because it was the place she died – but because it was the place I cleaned up her shit.* (The sin-eater had just listened and nodded, looking not like the fat, rollicking man who had sat at her table, looking like something spectral and unreal.) *And once you smell shit in a place, you smell it everywhere. Shit gets under your fingernails and never lets go.*

Twenty-three was possibly a little young for the menopause, but she had tested herself, and the test came up negative. But it was a fact: she hadn't menstruated since giving the sin-eater his meal.

Summer came and passed quick. She saw Lady Gaga in Rio with Fran and the emoji crowd, spent a month in the better part of Greece with a dashing young registrar she'd met through Johan, did weekenders in NYC and across the Pennines.

Although she now thought of webcamming as a thing of the past, she began again to document her life on social media, uploading YouTube fashion tutorials and pinterests and long, drunken, giggly podcasts with her girlfriends.

Then the autumn came, and brought bad news.

It came in the form of a skinny young man who approached her in the Bridge. He wore a beanie hat and the flustered expression of badly skilled criminals. He called her by name, and it took a beat for Lexi to remember who he was. Oh yeah: Kelly had an older brother called Liam, and this was him.

"Lex, how's it going?"

"I'm alright. Still drinking the pale ale?" Lexi nodded to his glass.

Liam sat down. He was eating some kind of roast panini from the van outside.

"Yeah, I heard you're the real gallivanter these days?"

"What can I say? I get around. And if you're gonna sit down, can you not drop salad and shit all over my magazine?"

"Sorry," said Liam. "Burger vans. My guilty pleasure."

Lexi hated that expression.

"So how you doing, anyway?"

Not like she cared. It was a while since she'd had to talk to anyone this dull.

"Not so well. Morrisons paid us off, then that went, had to move back in with the old girl. Jobcentre sanctioned me, and Mam's hassling us for non-dep charges."

"I'll give you fifty quid if you cut the sob story," Lexi said.

"Actually, Lex, I was thinking you could do a bit more than that. You're rich off that dinosaur game, and we both know that weren't your idea. As Kelly's grieving relative I deserve a cut, plus percentages."

"No way! The game was developed by the limited company. I was a co-director. You have no legal claim."

"Maybe not. But we both know you watched my sister die, fucked her boyfriend, got rich off her hard work. Maybe others should know. Maybe the papers'd be interested." Liam got up. "So if I was you, I'd keep your spare change."

She'd meant to be going to Calum and Dave's Headingley bash but had delayed it: she wanted some time alone to work this out. She took a glass of red wine and drew a long hot bath and took a shit. Twice a day this overwhelming need came upon her, but all she could produce at the bowel were these spatters of black rabbit droppings.

She lay in the bath and drank her wine and thought – what hurts isn't what he could do but the fact he *said* it. Formed words out of the regret she used to feel. This worst possible interpretation.

She made a carbonara, took it into the front room, flicked around on the TV until she found an old *Take Me Out* and munched down the carbonara, then ate a pack of mini crème eggs. *Guilty pleasures.* Another cliché. Another thing used most often about food. She finished her glass of wine and poured another. Yeah, Liam could spread lies in the papers, on Facebook and try to ruin her socially. All he could do. He wasn't getting any money – not that there was all that much left. The last time she had spoken to her financial adviser, just before the New York trip, he had told her that her capital was running low, the percentage deal hadn't been as good as she had thought, and the man had even advised her to think about 're-entering the workplace'.

I could do anything.

But Lexi couldn't imagine leaving the city. She was a gallivanter, like Liam had said – but she couldn't imagine herself *living* in London or Rio or New York, where she knew no-one.

It was that he actually said *it. Actually said it.*

I could kill him.

She finished her meal and turned off the TV. It was time to plan what she would wear to the party.

"No. I ain't doing it."

"I'm not asking you to do anything," Lexi said. "I'm just asking you to eat the sin."

The sin-eater shook his head. They were in the Royal Park and he was eating pork scratchings.

"It's an indulgence, a big one. I don't do indulgences. I know a guy who can handle it, mate of my brother's, but –"

"Then put me in touch."

"What you're proposing is a *mor*tal sin. It is murder."

"Come on. No-one's gonna miss a dipshit benefit claimant."

"I know the Hawk. It's a small estate and people don't generally leave. If this guy disappears the police are gonna notice."

"But you have power. You can protect me."

"No, I can't."

The sin-eater munched up his pork scratchings and Lexi watched him. Pork scratchings, the ultimate pub food, crunchy and wet and hard and soft all at once. How could you eat something like that?

"I cannot interfere with the laws of man. It's the Covenant. I already done enough. Look, there's stuff that's bigger than you or me. Your friend, Mr Day, he's a sick man. The wasting disease."

Lexi drank back a vodka and Coke. It was true that she hadn't seen Mark for a while – but this didn't matter now. The vodka had a cold, slimy taste, she suspected from an inferior supermarket brand.

"Well, damn lot of help you are."

"Hey, all I've ever offered is temporary ease and restment. I get in trouble enough for that. Sin is always with us. Not just the mortal and the venial but the sin of being alive, of despair and sadness and regret, what the Catholics call *original sin*."

"Whatever," said Lexi, and left.

She flagged down a cab outside Abu Bakr. When she got back Liam was already waiting outside her front door. He wore a town shirt and enough aftershave to stun a mountain lion.

"Good. You're here."

She opened the door and Liam Dales walked into the house as if he already owned it. The blackmailer walked into the front room – walking trainers all over Lexi's Pashtun rug she had picked up in Fifth Avenue – and peered at the DVDs.

"*Legally Blonde 2*? I never seen such shite."

"Well, you didn't come here to watch the movies," she

said – straining to get exactly the right note of stern flirtation into her voice. It was tricky because too much leg and cleavage would scream honeytrap, and yet he had to believe there was a chance. Her outfit for the evening had been carefully calibrated.

In the kitchen she poured two glasses of wine and carried them back on a serving tray. The tray also had a sheaf of documents. She sat down next to him and smoothed her skirt over her legs, with care. With her remote she turned on Lady Gaga.

"Prefer a beer, if you got one," said Liam Dales.

"Tonight you drink wine."

Dales shrugged and knocked back half the glass.

"Let's get down to it. What's the legal shit I got to sign?"

Lexi passed the papers to him. Liam gave them a cursory scan – no more – before signing them with Lexi's Parker pen. Lexi had used it to sign her co-directorship of Chromosal Tec, about a hundred years ago.

"Nice one. When do I get the money?"

"It's a straightforward transfer. Be in your account in four hours."

"Cheers, Lex." Liam stood up, then staggered. There was an alarming glazed look in his eyes.

"Sit down, arsehole."

Liam fell back onto the sofa.

"I always thought you was fit as all that. Like my sister. I wanted to fuck you both on the internet."

"Well, that's really sweet of you to say so."

She cupped his chin and forced more wine down his throat. He wasn't so good at keeping it in his mouth and some of the wine would have splashed over Lexi's new Sofaworks, had she not taken the precaution of putting an old blankie down.

"Come on, you fucking lightweight. Drink to your success."

"I think you killed Kelly, you bitch."

Lady Gaga was singing about how *you make me wonder why, I like it rough, I like it rough.*

"No way you would of had patience to deal with her for six month when she were ill. You had the drugs." He was laughing now. "You could of done it."

"I could have," said Lexi, "but I didn't."

It took another twenty minutes for Liam Dales to die. Lexi put *Gogglebox* on and burned the papers in the fire – useless anyway, she had just mocked something up on Microsoft Publisher. She had some wine from another bottle and got quite into the TV show. Fast-forwarding through a commercial break she glanced at Liam Dales and realised that he was no longer thrashing around or even breathing. She took his pulse. Nothing.

She picked up the phone. Now for phase two. Scatter some drug paraphernalia around and pass Dales off as an OD. The potassium would back this. There would probably not even be an inquest. Risky, and she had considered luring Dales somewhere outside – God knew Leeds had plenty of remote wilderness – but she couldn't handle the thought of spending all night digging a grave.

Lexi dialled three nines and a voice came on the phone. Instead of asking her which service she required, the voice said:

"Oh dear, Miss Blythe. A mortal sin. You were warned."

"Have I got the wrong number?"

"The Covenant has been broken." This new voice was hard-accented East London. "You better stay there, Miss Blythe."

And the phone clicked off.

Lexi spent another six minutes trying to get through to the emergency services. Her landline and both mobiles were dead, and the internet connection appeared to be down. She thought of running... but the idea of going out into that night, where the voice lived, was worse than staying in this house with her best friend's dead brother lying face down on the Pashtun rug.

Finally there came a knock at the door.

The man at the door was tall, robed, gaunt and grave – the way she had imagined the sin-eater would look. But he spoke like a friendly bailiff... a debt collector.

"Dear oh dear, Miss Blythe." The debt collector took off his hat and entered the hallway.

Lexi was thinking she needed to improve the quality of her house guests.

"Fuck me." The debt collector was looking at the body of Liam Dales. "This *is* awkward, isn't it? It's Dickie Munslow's fault. He's too old school. Like the idiot Nazarene himself, who thought he could make everyone feel good about themselves with his moronic sacrifice. Not that simple, is it, Miss Blythe?"

The debt collector had taken off Liam Dales's clothes and was setting about him with strange, old tools.

"What are you doing," she asked, and the debt collector began to tell her but instead of his voice she heard the voice of her mam, talking of the *original sin, got above yourself, being too clever, feed me, feed me now, because all pleasures must be guilty, or else*. The collector turned. He had Liam Dales draped over his shoulder in a fireman's lift.

"Where are you taking the body?" she asked.

"Nowhere," said the debt collector. "We're going to eat it."

Mating Week

RUBY COWLING

SHE RAISES THEM from eggs. The adults have a week of life to mate, lay eggs, and die. Last weekend, fourteen of them struggled at last from their cocoons, taking a pause for the blood to pump into their pale green wings, and took to the air. For the last two nights they've flitted around the storm lamps that light Sarah's moth house, making indoor lightning that crackles the cool air as she works. But tonight as she opens the back door and flicks on the switch, she sees all but one of the Luna moths have disappeared.

For months she anticipates these few nights of frantic, mysterious company. When they die, she usually finds bodies on the white gravel floor, down amongst the huddled pots of young birch and alder. She'll pick them up carefully by the tip of a foot, the bodies paper-crisp and somehow lighter than air, and carry them gently out to the garden on her palm to return them to the soil. Now, though, even kneeling with leaves catching in her hair, raking through the gravel to the underdirt, she finds nothing.

The moth house is how she thinks of the small extension, bracketed by her neighbours' clean glass conservatories, that juts into the tiny walled garden at the back of her terraced cottage. She made it herself from panels of black mesh stapled into balsa uprights. Beyond the garden end is a patch of urban wood: for a while an owl used to call from some high branch back there for hours and hours as Sarah worked. Then there were two, calling to each other, and then after a week or so she didn't hear them again.

She hatches the eggs, feeds the growing larvae and harbours the silent cocoons in a nursery area just inside the back door, and works wearing several jumpers and fingerless gloves at a wallpapering table against the brick back wall of the house, a bar heater at her feet when the night's cold enough. Her movements are so small as she works, sometimes with acrylics, sometimes oil, sometimes pencil: the moths come to rest for a moment on her hair. They're beautiful of course, in their short and glorious mating days, but her artistic interest is the fleshy little concertinas that are their caterpillars, and their long, secretive days of pupation.

Working at night in the moth house, she's free from the daytime jangle of the phone: her agent, her toddler-tied friends, the over-bright world inviting her to come and account for herself. Today, though, no-one phoned, and the four o'clock air grated with a silence so abrasive she was driven to kneel at the bookcase seeking the balm of poetry. *In my dreams I am always saying goodbye and riding away.* When Stevie Smith failed to calm her, she took out her mother's few bits of silver jewellery and the polish, and rubbed at them hard.

She leans into her drawing, uneasy now it's just herself and the one remaining moth who silently panics the air around the middle lamp. She is sketching a late larva, fat and spiny and masked with brown. She hopes that there may be eggs already, that at least there's been time for mating before the moths died. No bodies: they can't have died. So. But what, then? Her thoughts flit in small, stuck circles as she makes tiny pencil marks on the creamy paper.

Unsold works are propped six-deep against the studio wall. Her agent has started to get restless, phoning almost weekly.

"People want to look at nice things, I'm afraid," he says. "The looks on their faces when they see your stuff..."

"I know," she says. Her squirming, bristling larvae and ghostly crosshatched cocoons are not what people want on their walls. "I just – this is what I have to do at the moment."

"Darling, of course. But while you're in this little phase, how about some pretty ones of the butterflies themselves?"

She's told him *moths, not butterflies,* ten times already. She bites back the explanation and rings off.

Even she doesn't know why she's so involved with this subject – the barrier of the logical *why,* springing up unbidden, stops her even finishing a lot of these pieces – and she won't know until she gets to the end, whenever that might be.

The larva's almost-invisible hairs and toes make her squint, and her head aches by the time daylight comes. The phone rings in the kitchen. She's glad of the interruption, stretching her arms and massaging the back of her neck as she goes in.

The hello comes out properly on her second try.

"It's me," says the caller. "Oh, just a sec – "

Sarah can hear two small combative voices deep in the phone's aural space, their words tumbling over each other and over Melinda's entreaties: *nicely, Grace, let Oliver – shh, now that's not nice, give it to Mummy. Give. Grace. Oliver, stop it.* Everything in here is just as Sarah left it. She knows exactly how much milk there is in the fridge, and the battery in the wall clock still needs changing. The clock on the microwave says 08.07.

"Hi," comes a breathless voice in Sarah's ear, "What were you saying?"

"You rang me."

"Oh yes. Not too early, I hope? They were up at five today. Just wondering how you were, you know, and to remind you about tonight. *Oliver!*"

"Tonight." She eyes the calendar, which still displays the lilac-and-lemon posies of April. Flipping it over quickly, she realises today must be Thursday 5th, as there's a scribbled—

"Sec." Melinda's voice goes distant again as the two small voices rise.

—a scribbled note, Mel & Steve's 7pm. They want her to meet some work friend of Steve's, she remembers, and she suddenly feels tired.

Melinda comes back, "Sorry – I've got to go. See you about seven." And she puts down the phone before Sarah can say anything, not that there's a real need for her to say anything.

Sarah notices the kitchen bin needs emptying, counts nine mugs next to the sink. She must do something about the skirting board over there. Pulling on rubber gloves and swilling the fluffs of old tea down the sink, she hums, but the sound seems out of place and her throat is dry.

A life alone. Her mother used to use the phrase like a curse, but there's beauty in its assonance, its internal rhythm. It makes Sarah think of an owl's cry. She sees her friends *all the time*, she always assured her mother, though it's true that as they've staggered into their thirties and beyond it's become more difficult to fit socialising around the need to prepare lunchboxes and uniforms and get some sleep. Sarah is always pushing back a chair, saying goodnight, she must love them and leave them, get home to the studio and get something done. *I am glad, I am glad, that my friends don't know what I think.*

***

Night Waves is on the radio on the drive home. Steve's friend turns out to be a type her mother would have approved of; in spite of that, Sarah likes him. Scottish, graceful mover, steady eyes.

"Tell Ray about your paintings," Melinda had prompted as she carried a sleepy-eyed child up the stairs. Steve was clattering in the kitchen.

"Actually they're not paintings," was the first thing she'd said to Ray, correcting him for a mistake that wasn't even his. They talked a bit about her moths, and he made her laugh without her quite knowing how.

"I've never understood why you'd want to buy art just to look at it," he said, as they sat down to eat. "I mean, something that just looks like something. Why?"

Mel and Steve raised eyebrows at each other, fearing controversy, but Sarah felt a little leap, a freshness under her skin, and said:

"No, he's fair enough, if it just mirrors something, it's pointless."

He had hardly talked about himself in the usual curriculum vitae way, and hadn't asked her any of the usual questions about herself either, but it seemed already as if they were co-conspirators, kids who'd seek each other out in the playground. Mates. When he did talk about his own work, in computers, she was surprised how interested she was. Unlike Steve, he was happy at the company; Steve said – not for the first time – that his kids were his life, that work was just a means of feeding and clothing them, and Mel had nodded and squeezed his hand. Ray was working on something about *persistence*, which he said was a quality your data gains when you tell the machine to save, that is, make a record, until which point it doesn't exist; and although she didn't fully understand how his project was finessing this idea, the idea itself pricked her.

But Steve had leant in and quipped, "You'll need persistence with her," and then one of the children was heard padding around upstairs and since they'd finished dinner Mel took Sarah up to say a final goodnight – for they are fond of each other, Mel's children and Sarah – and they didn't go back to the topic.

***

As she was pulling on her coat after coffee, Ray asked for her number, and she gave it to him. But if he calls, she's not sure. It's a lot of trouble. You say you'll go for a drink and then after a few months you're sitting straight-spined on separate halves of the sofa blurting horrible gobs of truth at one another and someone starts crying, and it's back to square one.

Once she's pulled into her drive and roughly lined up with the letterbox on the front door she turns off the engine. There's silence and darkness and she takes this moment, as she likes to do, to savour the fact that no-one knows exactly where she is right now; it's as if she *isn't* here right now, and for a few heady seconds she is unchained from the world.

***

It's in a dream that night that she's back on her knees in the moth house. She pulls aside the drainage stones under the planters, finds nothing. She shoves through the lower leaves of the young birches, tipping the planters to climb further in. Then she sees something stuck to the underside of a large leaf, hanging there as incongruous as a third ear. It's a cocoon – a moth's – but it shouldn't be out here; she takes care of all those stages in her array of plastic pots and old cordial bottles in the nursery. It's also larger than normal: fatter than her forefinger and nearly as long. She sees another one clinging to a stem, and now look, there are a handful, a dozen. Another pupation is taking place; inside these cocoons the moths are remaking themselves a second time. There's a split in the first cocoon already and she can't resist; gently holding the leaf, she pulls a nail down the split and opens it up. Instead of the moist folds of a new moth, what's inside is dry and white. A scroll of paper. With her nail, she hooks it whole out of its brown shell and it drops to the ground. Her hands are shaking but she picks it up and unrolls it. On the paper are faint markings, not much more than whispers, but they form a familiar image; the most familiar image, in fact: the shapes and outlines of her own face.

***

When Ray hasn't phoned by Monday, Sarah gets restless, and then annoyed at that, like a bite on top of a bite. If she could admit it, which she can't, she'd say it was the old clamour for a mate, unwelcome and unhelpful and maddeningly compelling. Since the dream, she's flowing, finishing her drawings, but the quiet nights are making her shiver.

Starting her day, in the warm May glaze of 5pm, she takes more care than usual clipping new sprigs of leaves from the growing alders and misting the larvae's tubs with water. She's bothered by the frass on the sheet under the tubs, and she gathers up the sheet and presses it into the washing machine, adding the kitchen tea-towels. She hesitates, then goes upstairs and strips her bed. Turning to come backward down the stairs, she bends and sweeps away the rolls of dust step-by-step with a pillowcase.

Dustpan and brush come out, and a damp cloth and a pine spray and the hoover. By nine she's attacking the spiderweb corners of the moth house. She pushes a stepladder through the greenery and climbs to where roof mesh meets wall mesh at the wooden frame. The heat up here is surprising. It muffles things. Then she feels a slice of cool air moving the hair against her neck, like something whispering to her. She touches the skin where it's brushing, and follows the invisible rope of air to the shadowy panel of mesh in front of her. There's a hole. This is where they've been leaving. Her moths haven't been dying and disappearing; rather, they've been flying away from her to freedom: sensing the slim corridor of air by temperature or sound or some mysterious moth-knowledge – it was probably as obvious as a motorway to them – and taking this little doorway into the rest of the world. As they have every right, she supposes as she slowly retreats down the stepladder, to choose to do.

***

With the end of June come short working nights and a reckless abundance of daylight. Sarah knows she's losing nothing when, after some cautious texts followed by phone calls almost adolescent in length, she agrees to an evening picnic with Ray. She doesn't need so much of the night, anyway: the moth works she's finishing will be her last, and although she never perfected the pencil drawing of the caterpillar it was recognisable, at least; she got it down. There is something of hers to see, now. She has talked her agent into taking all her moth works for a joint exhibition later in the summer, and, maybe, she'll ask Ray to come to the opening. What she will show ought to be enough: her long-flown creatures in their former state, persisting, as if she still held them cupped precious in her hands.

The Bright Room

ANTHONY WATTS

She comes to the bright room as to a feast
of light. For as long as she's allowed
she'll bask in its shadowless glow. The room
is immense – bigger than the world. It contains
all there is to know. But most importantly
her friends are there. All of them. They chat
for hours. She doesn't want them to go. But one
by one they log off. See ya.
See ya.

Under the duvet
she holds herself small
and tight as a pip. Hiding
from the darkness in the darkness, she tries
to delete the night and its noises

the beat of her own heart

her father's footstep on the landing.

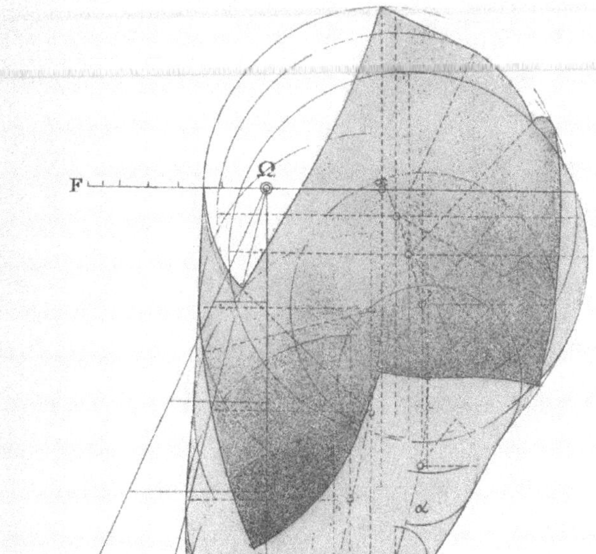
F
Ω
α
It
11·0
10·3

It

GAIA HOLMES

It made her want to drink the last of the Christmas sherry,
climb over the park railings after midnight
and cry at Adonis's feet.

It made him want to phone in sick
and spend the rest of the day in bed with her
eating treacle sponge and custard, playing chess.

It made them want to go to the next alcoholics anonymous
meeting.

It made him want to go to the woods
with a week's supply of cream crackers, tinned sardines
and his dead grandmother's fat three-stone bible.

It made him want to pull out his tubes,
curse at the nurses
and shuffle to the gardens to smoke a cigarette.

It made them want to adopt.

It made her want to touch his wife's breasts
to see if they were real.

It made them want to drive to the seaside on a rainy day,
park up on the cliff top, eat egg mayonnaise sandwiches,

drink tea from a thermos flask and watch the grey waves
curling and rolling through the steamy windows.

It made him want to apologise.
It made her want to murder.

It made her want to wear Doc Martens
and a chiffon dress the colour of ostrich steak.

It made him want to go to the library
and borrow a book on goat husbandry.

It made her want to paint all the windows with bitumen,
burn all his letters and cry for six weeks.

It made him want to eat fried rice with a pair of tweezers.

It made them want to slow-roast the placenta
in a casserole dish with Bisto, onions and leeks.

It made him want to pour treacle
into the toecaps of all his trainers.

It made him want to teach his Jack Russell how to iron.
It made her want to set fire to her Barbie doll's hair.

It made her want to move to Russia,
gorge on roast turnips and black bread
and become comfortably fat.

It made him want to stroke her clavicles.

It made her want to wear a fake moustache
at the wedding reception.

It made him want to curl up in a fist
at the bottom of her bed.

It made him want to steal a wedge of Brie
from Sainsbury's deli counter.

It made her want to sell her soul on eBay.

It made her want to try it when her parents were out.
It made him want to think about it for a long time in the bath.
It made them want to forget about it and get on with their
lives.

Concerning That Girl

P.R.

Does It make her cry at the number on the scales, again? Has It given her a never-ending list of unrealistic goals? Did she have another tough week? Were the days long and the nights longer? Does she believe It when It tells her she is a big fat disappointment? Has she ever tried to ignore It? What is the tone? Is the relentless commentary always so cruel? Is the girl glad to have It looking out for her?

Will the girl faint, again? It makes her pulse tired. Is the beat fading away? Does this frighten her? Will there be an audience this time? Will anyone help her? At which point will the soft-faced school nurse intervene? Has she seen It too many times? Will her forever-smile melt and give birth to a frown? Will her good heart sink? Does the girl see all this?

Is the girl incoherent, again? Does It make her mind cloudy? How long did It take to annihilate her old thoughts, the rational ones and nostalgic dreamtime? Have her A*s turned to downward Ds? Do her teachers worry? Is there a newish teacher who has seen a similar thing with his daughter? Did he cry and regret at the funeral? Could he have done more? Do they discuss It in the staffroom? Has anyone remembered to order the NHS info leaflets? Would the girl notice anyway?

Will the girl lie, again? Has It made her paranoid? Does she refuse to eat her mother's groceries? Does she worry that she is being tricked? Has she noticed her mother weep as she refuses to eat breakfast, lunch and tea? Did she see her throw a glass hard at the wall? Has It turned her compassion to fog? Has her conscience gone on standby, like most of her body? Does the girl care?

Does the girl admire her ailing body, again? Does she celebrate when another clump of hair glides from her balding head to the floor? Has she got enough sores and half-baked scars to parade? Is her immune system too floppy to fix them? Does she feel victorious to see her naked body and all Its hard work, all but jutting bones and a fine powdery down? Did this sprout in attempt to stop her constant shivering? Symptoms or medals? Is this indoctrination irreversible? Does the girl remember life before It?

Will the girl ignore her body screaming out for help, again? Will she ever realise she is poorly? Has she started to hear the whispers in the corridor? The muffled conversations at home, behind closed doors? The lingering stares from strangers on the street? Will the heart attack she is about to have be the end? Will It stop tormenting her before It slowly kills her? Or will she drag her weariness out of bed and cry at the number on the scales like always? Does the girl have the strength to fight Its pull?

Will the girl continue to deny Its existence, again? Does It have a name? Does she secretly call It Ana? Does she think if she calls It Ana It will be her friend? Has It made her forget what real friendship is? Does the girl call It Ana because deep down inside she knows Its real name?

Elephant

LEDLOWE GUTHRIE

It pushed our pillows apart and
though I wanted to
it dragged my head away
when you kissed me

It hunched your shoulders closed
filled your body with stones
pulled you into the darkness

From safe distances
conversations skirted
clung in corners
stretched along walls

Like a leech it swelled
sucked you dry and empty
a dusty lake bed

It swallowed your loud words
wrapped your voice in grass
so when we talked
it hid your sound from me

Then like the shedding
of a skin grown old
the unexpected turn of a season
You unfurled and breathed.

The Man Who Disappeared

SIOBHAN DONNELLY

IT MADE ITS way through the brain, destroying as It went. It saw the workings of the brain as a series of wires and laughed at how easy it was to unplug them. Sometimes It cut through them cleanly and quickly, a neat execution, killing the memory before anyone had time to remember It had been forgotten. Other times It dragged the death out, made it slow and painful, Its own unique form of torture. Sometimes It was picky about its food, choosing one memory over another. It had a particular taste for faces, previously it had been names.

In the beginning It lay low, not wanting to draw too much attention to itself, not until It had gathered its strength. To begin with the man didn't even realise It was there. It sent out Its scouts to explore the man's mind and search out the weak spots. Once It had gathered enough information It slowly began to flex Its talons and by the time the man began to notice the army invading his head it was too late; It had already taken hold and woven Its web too tightly for it to be broken.

Sometimes It made Its presence known through only the quietest of whispers, a forgotten name or a wrong turning. Other times Its greed would overwhelm and It would swell in size until It engulfed everything. The blackness in the man would expand until he no-longer knew where or who he was. It made him lost within himself. On other occasions, instead of withholding information, It would overload the brain with a tsunami of material: thousands upon thousands of memories, thoughts, images, facts, voices, faces; a dizzying mass of information; haircut at half past three get sausages from Dales Wildman Street dinner with Anne second house on the right with a blue door the 567 bus don't be late the taste of salt in the sea air new shoes for his birthday walk the dog feed the cats pay the electricity bill Christmas '85 in Dumfries his mother shouting for him to come downstairs his wife shouting for him to come upstairs the children shouting for him to come and play with him in the garden Carol's face coming closer and closer her eyes shining where did he leave the car didn't he sell the car when did he sell the car on, and on it went, never stopping. The befuddlement this never ending stream of thought caused the man made It laugh at Its own wicked cleverness.

***

It followed the man into the kitchen one afternoon. The man was hungry but couldn't remember if he had eaten lunch or not. The pile of dirty plates in the sink suggested that he had so he surmised that he just needed a small snack to tide him over until teatime, whenever that would be. Time confused him these days. He picked up a banana from the fruit bowl and that's when It decided to play a game with him. As the man turned the banana over in his hands to ascertain that it wasn't still green, he became perplexed and suddenly could no longer remember how he was supposed to eat the fruit. He passed it back and forth between his hands struggling to remember. He knew some fruits like oranges needed to be peeled before you could eat them, yet with others like apples and pears one simply bit into it, skin and all, but of bananas he could not recall. It enjoyed the man's uncertainty and let the image of the apple linger at the forefront of his mind until the man decided the peel was meant to stay on and took a large bite out of the fruit. The peel's waxy texture turned almost powdery as it made contact with the man's tongue. It was tasteless, yet somehow sharp, drying out his mouth in the way that the acidity of a gooseberry will do, and left an unpleasant and lingering aftertaste on his tongue. As the man spat out the banana skin, his face contorted with disgust; It was beside Itself with laughter. After a few moments spent struggling to work out how to peel the fruit, the man finally succeeded and paced up and down the kitchen, slowly chewing the banana. Once he had finished, he stood holding the banana peel in front of him unsure whether he was meant to keep it or throw it away. Uncertain, he resolved to wait until his mind felt clearer and to make the decision then. He placed the banana skin in the breadbin for safe keeping and left the kitchen.

***

It enjoyed watching the man search for a memory that was no longer there, watching him reach out desperately for the names of people and places. It enjoyed taunting him, dangling the thought just out of reach, edging it towards him and snatching it away. It made trying to hold onto memories like trying to keep a firm grip on a bar of soap with wet hands. More often than not, like the soap, the memories would gaily slip from the man's fingers and slide down the plughole.

There were days when It seemed to have disappeared and the man's mind worked almost as well as it had in his youth. His brain would spring back into colourful life, words flowed freely, names matched faces, and the man would tentatively begin to wonder if perhaps this time It was gone for good. But inevitably It would return. It would wake from Its hibernation with renewed energy, returning with greater force than ever before and usually with some new cruel trick It had learnt and would mercilessly test out on the man. It made the man think he was young again. It played him memories from his youth, working down the docks, drinking with friends, meeting his wife, holding his new-born son for the first time. Some days It would make the man forget who he was.

One morning It led the man over to the high bay windows at the front of the house, where the window cleaner was just finishing up his work. The window cleaner was an elderly man; his face was thin, drawn, and covered in a layer of greying skin that hung loosely from his cheekbones like an oversized piece of cloth. The man was surprised he was able to work, his movements as slow and seemingly painful as they were. Realising he was being watched the window cleaner beckoned for the man to open the window, presumably to discuss payment or arrange a future booking. The man fumbled with the catch and after a few failed attempts succeeded in opening the window. A light breeze wafted through the newly created space bringing with it the scents of spring and filling the man with a welcome sense of contentment. He greeted the window cleaner cheerfully and enquired how he could help but the window cleaner merely stared back at the man as though waiting for him to say something more. The man began to repeat the question but as soon as he did the window cleaner began talking. The man paused and so did the window cleaner. The man tried again and the same thing happened. Despite his usually calm nature the man was beginning to get annoyed. He made a further attempt to find out what the odd old man wanted but once again the window cleaner talked straight over him, he too sounding increasingly annoyed. At this point the man lost his temper; the window cleaner should know better than to play such foolish and childlike games. It was something he wouldn't even expect of his own grandchildren and he told him as much. To the man's ever increasing annoyance the window cleaner didn't appear to register the man's comments as he was too busy shouting his own insults back through the window. By now the man was angry and confused; he'd only opened the window because the other man had asked him to and now he was caught up in some kind of ridiculous argument with a man he didn't know. He finally lost his temper and began to shout at the other man. To his displeasure the window cleaner responded in kind, becoming ever more vocal and animated, hurling a barrage of insults towards the man.

The garden surrounding the window cleaner began to change; the world became distorted as colours merged together and fragments of the garden seemed to disappear and float away. The window cleaner's shouts became louder and louder until they no longer sounded like words but an unbearable roar that filled the man with an overwhelming sense of fear. Then as quickly as it had started, it was over. There was no window cleaner; there wasn't even a window, simply an old man shouting at his own unfamiliar reflection, a reflection that stared back at him with a face filled with confusion. It had fooled him once again.

***

When It was feeling particularly strong It would break Its way out of the brain and venture forth to new playing fields, untouched land It would claim for its own and lay waste to, where it could wage its war and conquer the body. As It took control of them, one by one the man's fingers began to work against him. They refused to do the simplest of the man's biddings and often he couldn't even remember what it was he wanted them to do. The craftsman quickly disappeared to be replaced by a man who struggled to tie his own shoe laces.

In the garden was a crumbling outhouse that functioned as a utility room, just large enough to fit in a washing machine and tumble dryer. On washing day the man would amble to and fro between the backdoor and the outhouse carrying bundles of laundry, first to the washer, then to the dryer, and finally back inside to be ironed. Now he lived alone it was a much smaller task than it used to be, but the man liked this routine and habits like this helped him feel as though he was in control. It had noticed this and was displeased. It watched one day as the man carried the laundry basket back into the house and set it down on top of the kitchen table. It watched as the man sorted through the basket pairing socks and folding underpants. It watched as the man retrieved the ironing board from the cupboard under the stairs and brought it through into the kitchen. And then It struck.

As the man tried to set up the ironing board his fingers lost their grip and the object fell from his grasp. Bending down to retrieve it, the object suddenly became unfamiliar to him and he could no longer see how to manoeuvre the criss-crossed legs into a position that would let the ironing board stand up. The man tried to pull one of the legs so that it was at a right-angle to the top of the board, but this only forced the other leg into a horizontal position which confused him further. The man made various attempts to get the ironing board to stand with diminishing success. At one point he managed to slot the holding bar into one of the grips but when he stood it up the board only came up to his knees. Exasperated, the man tried to alter the board's height but he couldn't remember how he'd got it to stand in the first place and his fingers were refusing to grip properly. Losing patience with it, the man began to haphazardly push and pull at the thing, wrenching it until, with an unpleasant grating sound, the legs jammed. The man swore in frustration and aimed a sharp kick at the ironing board. As the pain shot through his foot, the man's frustration bubbled into anger until, with an amount of strength that took even It by surprise, he lifted the ironing board above his head and threw it across the width of the room where it crashed into the wall and broke.

The man stood panting for a while. His head felt as though it was full of smoke. His thoughts clouded; he was unable to remember what he had been doing or why his arms ached so much. The man gazed around the kitchen blankly looking for something that would jump start his memory and explain to him what he was doing. Curious, It held back any clues, waiting with interest to see what the man would do next. The man's eyes came to rest on the laundry piled up on kitchen table; he smiled to himself confident that he had remembered now. He crossed the room and scooped the clothes back into the laundry basket and headed out of the backdoor towards the outhouse.

As he closed the outhouse door behind him, the man could hear the whoosh of the water as it filled the drum of the washing machine. He was overcome with a sense of satisfaction and achievement, confident that this time It hadn't won.

In the kitchen, the ironing board lay broken on the floor.

***

As It grew stronger It began to alter the world around It. It made the familiar, unfamiliar and the new, terrifying. It took the street map in the man's head and jumbled it up, moving landmarks and changing street names. Once familiar journeys became never-ending mazes in which he would remain trapped for hours, retracing his steps over and over again, confusing left from right and going around in circles. Sometimes this could happen without the man even having to move. It distorted the man's perception and regularly made him lose his footing. It began to play with time. It made the days stretch on for months and years fly by in seconds. For all the man knew the birth of his daughter could have happened fifty years ago or merely five days ago.

In the very early days of Its attack, back when the man had first become aware of It, he had sought help from doctors. They sent him away with a myriad of pills and vague, non-committal assurances of confidence that their prescriptions would keep It at bay. For a short time the medication appeared to have an effect. The chemicals confused It. It hadn't prepared for a counterattack and for a while It was forced into hiding. The man felt lighter in body and mind. He rejoiced in being able to return to a sense of normality and congratulated the doctors on their excellent concoction of drugs, but it was not to last. Soon It learnt how to work its way around them and they stopped being effective. After a time they told the man not to take the pills. It had become too strong for them to be able to work anymore. They were a waste of his time and a waste of their money. They exchanged the pill boxes for removal boxes and moved the man out of his home into a different sort of home, a home with locked doors and set meal times.

***

It was triumphant in Its victory and celebrated by testing out Its latest trick. In Its last and final act of cruelty, It started to make the man fade away. As with everything It did, It began slowly at first. It made the man disappear for seconds, then minutes, and then when It was confident no-one had noticed, hours at a time. Soon there were days when the man didn't seem to be there at all, It smothered him and replaced him with a stranger. A stranger that was unable to do anything for himself. A stranger that would scream and lash out when approached. A stranger that spent his days rattling locked door handles, trying to get out in time to collect his children from school. A stranger who spent his nights crying for the mother he thought had forgotten him.

Then one day It won and the man disappeared altogether.

The Iolaire

AILEEN SHIRRA

It stole the flower of our island,
that distant war.
Full of *joie de vivre,* and bravado of youth
they left, right fine and bold,
fresh from heather covered fells,
the tang of peat smoke in their clothes,
and returning, so few survivors,
some seemed... no, not just old
but defeated, those victors
dragging ragged limbs, a breath from home,
aboard the teeming Iolaire,
with haunted eyes or startled rabbit gaze
drowning in images unbidden
of shrieking shells blooming bloody
in the fields of France
or flowering in the foaming seas.
A few would have sacrificed those limbs
to purge these horror-ridden reels
in the dying hours of that deadly year

But here no deathly shower descended,
lashing down from a queasy sky,
and then such joy! In the lee of Lewis Isle
with surely nothing left to fear
except the memories,
the nightmare memories

...and aye, perhaps the realisation
of all that had been lost
and all that yet may stray
across the eyes of loved ones
welcoming these draggled strangers.
Oh was there ever such an irony as this?
To lose their youth,
to leave their blood
pooling in the trenches of the Western Front
but haul their bodies home... to die,
the heart ripped from the Iolaire,
ravaged by the tearing teeth and claws
of the brutal Beasts of Holm

It stole the flower of our island that distant war...
But a few precious petals washed home on the swell of a New
Year tide

It

SHAWNI DUNNE

IT DOESN'T KNOW why it follows him, but it does. It clings to his heels, crawls over cracks in concrete, scrambles up walls just to be with him. It stands beside him when the rain soaks through it, when the wind flurries leaves and litter across it and when the sun makes it visible, definite, defiant. These are the days it likes the most. When he almost notices it. When he raises his hand to shade his eyes and it can drape Itself across him, feeling the warmth of his body, his steady breathing.

In the long nights it fades to nothing, merging with the darkness that seeps in through the curtains. It is the undeath, the pre-life, the void. Anything is possible. Sometimes he turns in his sleep, rolling over so that his face becomes masked in moonlight. It feels itself becoming real, edges forming where there was only silence and air. It glides over the bedsheets and breathes him in, their lips almost touching, before he turns away and it is gone, thrown violently from this world.

In those hours it waits, patiently, concealed by gloom but always watching. It watches minutes pass, then hours, but the passing of time means nothing to it. It had lived this way for many years. It could live this way forever. The boundless stretch of limbo is worth it for that moment when the sun rises and casts an orange glow that fuses them together, united, as one. In the night he is free but in the daylight, he can't escape.

It had perfected its act when it was small. It was performance; it was art. It was the most elegant dancer, a beautiful mime, and its movements were as light as air, flowing from him to it in fluid motion. Their fingertips dance together. A divine duet.

It remembers many years ago how he would hold his hands out in front of his bedroom wall and laugh with joy and wonder at the illusions that it created. How it was revered! How it was loved. It held a magic power that no other could rival. Together they were unbreakable.

Now it is forgotten. Sometimes it tries to wave, tries with all its strength but he just doesn't notice it anymore.

With her it is all ravens and martinis and roses and lies. It hates her. It loathes her. She has become nestled inside him like a rot, a disease growing within. It tries to pull her away but she slips through its fingers, red hot to the touch, burning bright with venom. It tried to speak with *her* it, to tell it to go, to leave, to run away but it is dead. Nothing but a dead corpse looped around her ankle. She drags the carcass across the floor as she moves. Her footsteps are murder.

It is becoming obsolete. It is dying. It spends every day with the corpse now, staring at the blank eyes and rotting limbs. They are too close. She never leaves. It can feel the corpse's waxy skin against its own. Its nails are sharp and pointed. It's worse when they have to kiss, its lips against the cold, dead flesh. In the nights It is glad it is dust.

When she leaves it's a miracle. Light floods back into the house. It wants to run and dance around the streets but he just sits in silence. He holds his head in his hands. Some days he doesn't stop crying. The sound is unbearable, but the laughter is worse. It's then that it starts to notice that their fingertips don't quite touch, not anymore.

The days become longer. It follows him through corridors of iodine, white washed buildings, desperately trying to keep up, desperately trying to hold on. The world is on fast-forward. Everything is a blur. She's back and worse than ever. It feels itself fading when she's there. It can't breathe. It can't hear. Everything is losing colour.

It is laying with him, their arms lazily overlapping on the rough yellow blankets, when it catches her looking at it. It notices her eyes are nothing but empty sockets. "Do you believe in good and evil?" she asks him, climbing onto his lap, forcing it to fade, digging her knees into its chest, the corpse sliding across the bedframe. It notices that her long black dress is made of souls, swirling and screaming wordlessly. For the first time in its life it tries to pull away, to break the bonds, to move without him. But it is paralysed, bound by unseeing cords that dig painfully into its skin as it rips away. It feels sinews snap and veins burst; bones crunch under the pressure. It never knew It was so alive.

Her earrings are blood red rubies. It sees them reflected in her scythe.

When it looks at him it sees that he is fading too. His skin is translucent and cold to the touch. Maps of veins across his chest lead to nowhere. There is no pulse, no beat, no warmth. When it tries to reach out to him, it feels itself being dragged backwards through the air, as if pulled by a great current. It is over. It is done.

And then it feels the bindings break. There's a moment of pure fear and ecstasy, of confusion, a sense of falling and then it lashes out blindly, striking her.

She falls back in slow-motion, the souls flaring up around her, the scythe crumbling into ash. It closes its eyes, tinnitus rising, the chaos of the world crashing around it. Behind its eyes it sees a new world, beyond its own where unseen creatures roam on the fringes of reality. When it dares to look again, she is gone. It climbs up onto the bed beside him, shaking on newborn splintered limbs, and begins the tender and gentle work of connecting the broken bones and torn muscles, arteries and cartilage, sewing them back together again.

Tutorial

WILLIAM THIRSK-GASKILL

It made B lie on the floor before school, looking at the same
page of a textbook, for as long as time allowed.
It made B search the drawers in C and D's bedroom.
It made D ask C if it was time for C to have a talk with B,
which C did.
It made B suggest a question to the other children in the
street.

Its consequences were what prompted E's lifelong love of cats.

It made B miss a double Applied Maths lesson in order to go
home with F, while B's parents were at work.
It made F tell something to B, which B found hard to believe,
and which, after two weeks of recriminations, turned out
not to be true.
It made F move to Birmingham, and get a job with Severn
Trent Water.

G told B that she didn't want anything to do with it, which
was one reason why they split up when the next World Cup
came around.

It made H spend hours searching the internet, and years on
the Atkins diet.
It was one of the things that made H try to persuade B to stop
drinking alcohol.

It made H order pills from the USA that you can only get on prescription in this country, and which H later regretted taking.
It made B have to leave his office at lunchtime, and get to the laboratory within 20 minutes.
It made H keep the date of each attempt in her diary, and Polaroid micrographs on the mantelpiece.

It made J glad when K left, after L was born.

It made B write stories to read to L at bedtime.
It made B glad that L saw him win the air guitar competition at CenterParcs.
It made J and B fly to Kiev, twice, to no avail.

It made J give L frequent lectures, usually before L went out in the evening.

It was why B didn't mind putting up with E's cats when they got married.

About The Authors

Liam Brown is a writer and dancer from Birmingham, England. He is the author of two novels, *Real Monsters* and *Wild Life*. His third novel, *Broadcast,* is out mid-2017 on Legend Press.

Poppy Connor-Slater has been working on her first novel since graduating from the University of Huddersfield with an MA in Creative Writing. She spent much of her childhood reading myths and fairy tales and hopes to spend her adulthood writing them.

Matilde Christensen is the author of 'Greyhound', a short story inspired by the killing of Tim McLean in Canada in 2008, and the release of his murderer, Vincent Li, in 2015. Matilde grew up in Copenhagen, Denmark and moved to London at age 20. She now lives in Manchester, spends a lot of her time travelling and crafting, and aspires to one day write a lengthy novel about the madness and grotesque beauty of life.

Alexandra Davis lives in Suffolk. Her poems have been published in *Agenda, Artemis, The Fenland Reed,* in several Tanka publications, and by The Emma Press in *Slow Things* and *An Anthology of Love* (forthcoming). She has been commended in six competitions, including Ver and Ware Poets, and was a runner-up in the Mother's Milk Books Pamphlet Prize 2016. Visit www.alexandrapoet.wordpress.com.

Jennifer Gledhill moved to Huddersfield in 2011 to study English Literature and creative writing at the University of Huddersfield. She completed her MA by Research in 2016. She has no hobbies but, when asked in job interviews, lies and says she likes cooking and team sports.

Tracy Fells has won awards for both fiction and drama. Her short stories have appeared in *Firewords Quarterly* and *Popshot* magazine, online at *Litro New York, Short Story Sunday* and in anthologies such as *Fugue, Rattle Tales* and *A Box of Stars Beneath the Bed.* Competition success includes short-listings for the Commonwealth Writers, Willesden Herald, Brighton and Fish Short Story prizes. She shares a blog with The Literary Pig (http://tracyfells.blogspot.co.uk/) and tweets as @theliterarypig.

Wes Lee lives in New Zealand. Her poems have appeared in *The London Magazine, Poetry London, Magma, Westerly, The Best New British and Irish Poets 2015,* and many other journals and anthologies. She is the author of *Cowboy Genes* (Grist Books, 2014), *Shooting Gallery* (Steele Roberts, 2016), and a pamphlet forthcoming in 2017 with Eyewear Publishing in London. She was the 2010 recipient of the BNZ Katherine Mansfield Literary Award, New Zealand's foremost award for the short story. Most recently she was placed in *The London Magazine* Poetry Prize 2015, and The Troubadour Prize 2014.

Olivia Randall is a 22 year old Creative Writing postgraduate who enjoys romantic movies, long walks on the beach, and overused dating site clichés. 'Space Diving' is the first in a collection of otherworldly short stories, all of which feature elements of magic realism or new weird. The collection takes the normal, the mundane or the outright depressing and turns them into the ethereal and the bizarre. When she's not writing stories that upset her mum, Olivia reviews books and hosts creative writing events at pretentious bars.

L. F. Roth has had stories published in competition anthologies by Biscuit Publishing (2011), Earlyworks Press (2012, 2013, 2014, 2016), Bridge House Publishing (2014, 2015), Cinnamon Press (2016), AudioArcadia.com (2016) and Momaya Press (2016). They generally focus on relationships, gender issues and trauma.

Andrew McDonnell writes poetry and short fiction, the most recent appearances being the journal, *Butcher's Dog* and anthology, *Being Dad*. He lives in Norwich but works in Peterborough so that he can have a long commute and write stuff. He is an editor at Lighthouse Literary Journal.

Claire Martin lives in France and works in Paris in a lawyer's firm. She graduated from the University of Glasgow with an M Lit in Creative Writing and is currently working on a novel.

Martin Nathan has worked as an engineer on a number of major projects, including the Jubilee Line Extension, Terminal Five and CrossRail.

His short stories have appeared in a range of publications and on competition shortlists, including Cromagnon, HISSACS, the Bristol Short Story Prize, The Short Story prize and the Women in Comedy Award.

His novel *A Place of Safety* is to be published by Salt Publishing in 2018.

J. H. Lewis was born in Leicester and comes from a mixed Irish, English and Welsh working class background. During the 80s and 90s he became involved in the politics and the Troubles in Northern Ireland. These experiences have heavily influenced his writing. More recently he has spent time in the Eastern Cape of South Africa working with teachers on English Language projects in poor rural communities. He's written six novels.

Mark Kenny studied Biology at the University of Sheffield and works as a web developer for a telecommunications company. He has written short stories most of his life and is currently working on his first novel.

Michael Hargreaves is a lover not a writer. Originally from the sunny slums of Wigan, he is now nearing the end of a degree in English Literature at the University of Huddersfield. His story 'The Fear of Your Own Reflection' offers a taste of things to come as he continues work on his first novel.

Russell Reader won first prize in the *New Writer* magazine's Prose and Poetry Awards, 2014 for his short story 'The Lonely Toothbrush'. He has been shortlisted in *Fish Publishing, Words with Jam* and *Creative Writing Matters* competitions, and long-listed for BBC Radio 4's *Opening Lines*. He has also been highly commended by *InkTears*, and is a Flash 500 winner. He has previously been published by *Litro* and the University of Chester's *Flash Magazine*. He lives in Keele, England.

Jo Hiley lives on the 10th floor of a high rise block in Sheffield. She started writing about six years ago after joining a WEA writing class. She's currently working on a collection of short stories with a common theme of darkness and humour running through them. Most days she only has to look outside her window for inspiration.

John Beresford is currently working on a sequel to his second novel – *Gatekeeper* – published in 2015. His first – *War of Nutrition*, an eco-thriller about genetically modified foods gone wrong – was published in 2012. His radio play "Breakages Must Be Paid For" was long-listed for the BBC's Alfred Bradley Bursary Award in 2009.

Faye Chambers is a writer and musician from Elland, West Yorkshire. She is currently undertaking an MA researching sexual humour in the workplace. 'Michael, 38' is her debut as a published author. In between lurking in guitar shops and investigating dirty jokes you can find her at afayewithwords.wordpress.com

John Rathbone Taylor took up fiction writing to help him mentally shred all the plans and reports he used to write as a director in local government. Most of his work is thus in the nonsensically comedic yet deadly-serious style known as the bizarro or absurd. In contrast, 'Cairo Salutes' is John's first published story in what he terms the "extra-ordinary ordinary".

Ford Dagenham prefers his movies 90mins long with a linear narrative. He posts a poem or pic a day in his blog 'Hatchbacks on Fire'. This will continue until he dies or doesn't. He's fooling himself he speaks French impeccably.

Obviously he feeds the cat and has his own mass. He misses stuff from the olden days. Like alchemy and glass Lucozade bottles. His chapbook *A Canvey Island of the Mind* is available from Blackheath Books. His work is in *PUSH* and *Paper&Ink* zines. Faced with dilemmas he often runs a bath.

Erinna Mettler is a Brighton-based writer. She is a founder and co-director of The Brighton Prize for short fiction and of the spoken word group Rattle Tales. Her stories have been published internationally and short-listed for The Manchester Fiction Prize, The Bristol Prize, The Fish Prize and The Writers & Artists Yearbook Award. Her career highlight was having a short story read by a *Game of Thrones* actor at Latitude Festival. Erinna's new short story collection on the theme of fame, *Fifteen Minutes*, will be published by Unbound in 2017.

Gordon Williams was born near Manchester when the M6 was still cobbled. He moved to Northern Ireland in 1984 for the peace and quiet and, intractably indolent, still lives there. His first articles were published in sports magazines, none of which are still in business. His short stories have been published in magazines and anthologies, and on walls and websites. Some have won prizes in story competitions; most haven't. The "A" in his Creative Writing MA has been very useful when playing Scrabble with the letters after his name. As a part-time recluse looking to go full-time he has no presence on social media.

Max Dunbar lives in West Yorkshire. He blogs at http://max-dunbar.wordpress.com/ and tweets at http://twitter.com/MaxDunbar1.

Ruby Cowling was born in Bradford and lives in London. Her work has won *The White Review* Short Story Prize and the London Short Story Prize, and been shortlisted in contests from *Glimmer Train, Short Fiction,* and *Aesthetica*. Recent publication credits include *Lighthouse; The Letters Page; The Lonely Crowd; Unthology*; the Galley Beggar Press Singles Club; *I Am Because You Are* (a Freight Books collection of work inspired by the theory of General Relativity); and *Flamingo Land and Other Stories* (Flight Press). She is Associate Editor at *Short Fiction* and *The Writing Disorder*, and is a Spread the Word Associate Writer.

Anthony Watts has been writing 'seriously' for 45 years and has had poems published in magazines and anthologies in addition to four published collections: *Strange Gold* (KQBX Press, 1991), *The Talking Horses of Dreams* (Iron Press, 1999), *Steart Point & Other Poems* (John Garland, 2009) and *The Shell Gatherer* (Oversteps, 2011). He has won prizes in poetry competitions and his poems have been broadcast on BBC Radio 4 and Somerset Sound.

Gaia Holmes is a free-lance writer and creative writing tutor who has worked with schools, universities, libraries and other community groups throughout the Yorkshire region. She runs 'Igniting The Spark', a weekly writing workshop at Dean Clough, Halifax. She has had two full length poetry collections published by Comma Press: *Dr James Graham's Celestial Bed* (2006) and *Lifting The Piano With One Hand* (2013).She is currently working on her third collection which will, amongst other things, deal with gaps, sink holes, taxidermy and broad beans.

P.R. is a short story writer inspired by the life-challenges of ordinary people.

Ledlowe Guthrie lives in the green city of Sheffield. She writes plays and poetry and short stories, some of which, she is delighted to note, have been published and performed. She is thrilled to be included in the second Grist Anthology.

Siobhan Donnelly is the author of 'The Man Who Disappeared', the opening story in a collection of the same name. Inspired by her work in the care sector, this collection is an exploration of ageing and dementia. Since completing her MA, Siobhan has continued to work as a community artist running both writing and singing workshops. She is a co-founder of the *Umbrella Collective*, aiming to connect writing leaders across Kirklees and beyond. She has recently launched the *Letters Home* project, writing love letters to a past life.

Aileen Shirra was born and raised in Central Scotland and has worked in Adult Education throughout her working life, with the last 13 years spent as a Literacies Development Worker. This has allowed her to develop and enjoy her own love of reading and writing as well as supporting others to maximise their skills in these areas. She has had a variety of work, although mainly poetry, included in multi author publications and her first individual collection, *The Tumbrel of Time* was published in 2013 by Thynks Publications Ltd.

Shawni Dunne is from Wakefield, West Yorkshire. Shawni graduated from the University of Huddersfield in 2014, and is now studying towards a PhD at the university. As well as creative writing, Shawni is also interested in academic writing and has recently had an article published in *Cultural Intertexts*, an interdisciplinary journal under the aegis of Dunarea de Jos University of Galati, Romania.

William Thirsk-Gaskill prefers to describe himself as, 'devoting his whole time to writing' rather than, 'unemployed'. Sometimes, he receives 2-figure sums for his performances on the West Yorkshire spoken word circuit. His debut poetry collection, *Throwing Mother In The Skip* is published by Stairwell Books. His collection of short fiction, *Something I Need To Tell You*, also from Stairwell Books, should be coming out in 2017.

ABOUT GRIST

Grist offers a valuable platform for new writers. By publishing emerging writers alongside some of the more established names in literature, Grist offers an exciting opportunity for those starting out in their writing careers.

ACKNOWLEDGEMENTS

With thanks to our editorial team and to our judges Steve Ely, Steve Finbow, Helen Mort and Sam Jordison.

Special thanks are also due to Megan Taylor for her patience and good humour throughout the whole process, and to my colleague Michael Stewart for guidance and advice.

Many thanks to the University of Huddersfield for their continuing support.